WHAT TEENS ACTUALLY BELIEVE ABOUT JESUS
BASED ON NATIONAL RESEARCH

THE
JESUS
GAP

JEN BRADBURY
FOREWORD BY ANDREW ROOT

Eye-opening. Blood-chilling. Galvanizing. These were my reactions as I read the results of Jen Bradbury's research on the Jesus gap in youth ministries. Her findings regarding what teenagers and their parents believe about Jesus call upon us as youth workers to deeply reflect on our ministries, and they should provoke us to action. Jen does an excellent job of laying out the issues, as well as providing practical steps to address those issues and implement change in our ministries and churches. This should be required reading for every youth pastor, seminary student, senior pastor, and Christian parent.

Ginny Olson
Youth Ministry Author, Advocate, Advisor, and Adjunct Professor
Director of Youth Ministries for the Northwest Conference of the Evangelical Covenant Church

Jen Bradbury is seasoned, wise, and warm, as might be expected of a youth minister. She's also a tenacious researcher with mad writing skills and a desperately important problem to dissect. That's why *The Jesus Gap* managed to exceed my expectations. This book needs serious attention from anyone who loves Jesus, loves kids, and loves the church. There's hope in these pages!

Dave Rahn
Sr. VP, Youth for Christ/USA
Director, MA in Youth Ministry Leadership at Huntington University

What we think teens know about Jesus and what they actually know are often two very different things. In *The Jesus Gap*, Jen Bradbury sets out to discover what her students are learning, which spurs a much larger exploration of the Christologies of teenagers across the church. This book doesn't stop there, however. Through her own research findings, stories from years in youth ministry, and numerous creative teaching ideas, Jen offers practical ways for youth ministers to help young people meet Jesus. Yes, the gap is significant, but these pages are packed with wisdom, grace, and hope for anyone who loves Jesus and cares about teens.

Bethany Stolle
Designer, Educator, and the Curriculum Developer Behind
Sparkhouse Youth Ministry Resources (re:form, Connect)

The Jesus Gap is a must-read book for four reasons. First, it discovers, critiques, and champions the place of Christology in youth ministry. Second, it is a rare gem: National research done with rigor that helps us find a confident way forward. Third, it was written by a veteran youth pastor with a proven and current record of fruitful leadership. Finally, Jen Bradbury is a gifted thinker and leader in youth ministry who leads, teaches, and nurtures as well as any I've seen. You can be confident of the quality of the data, the theological wisdom, the practical application, and the integrity and Christ-centeredness of the one who writes.

Terry Linhart, PhD
Author and Educator at Bethel College – Indiana
TerryLinhart.com

In *The Jesus Gap*, Jen Bradbury offers deep insight into the way teenagers view Jesus. Full of important questions and a critical look at what we are telling teens about him, Jen offers a wealth of practical ways we can positively impact what our youth believe about Jesus. Regardless of your denomination or the size of your ministry, this book is filled with valuable wisdom for how pastors or parents can play a key role in strengthening the faith of our youth. I am left feeling hopeful that when we introduce teenagers to the true Jesus, we will open the door to a faith that will last a lifetime.

Doug Fields
Author of *Purpose Driven Youth Ministry* and *Your First Two Years in Youth Ministry*
Co-Founder of DownloadYouthMinistry.com

The Jesus Gap is thoughtful and compelling. With great skill and deep love, Jen grieves the loss of Jesus in the spirituality of teenagers and offers a hopeful vision of how the whole church can embrace a more robust Christology alongside students. It's time to invite Jesus back to youth group, and *The Jesus Gap* is preparing the way.

Morgan Schmidt
Youth Pastor and Author of *Woo*

The Jesus Gap is a powerful exposé on the perspectives of American "Christian" teens regarding the person of Jesus Christ. This is a must-read for anyone who is passionate about leading teenagers into a deep relationship with Jesus.

Dr. Steve Gerali
Award-Winning Author and Internationally Recognized Expert in Adolescent Development and Youth Ministry

The Jesus Gap
Copyright © 2014 by Jen Bradbury

Publisher: Mark Oestreicher
Managing Editor: Laura Gross
Editor: Tamara Rice
Cover Design: Adam McLane
Layout: Adam McLane
Creative Director: Alfred E. Neuman

ISBN-13: 978-1-942145-02-8
ISBN-10: 1942145020

The Youth Cartel, LLC
www.theyouthcartel.com

Email: info@theyouthcartel.com

Born in San Diego
Printed in the U.S.A.

To Doug, who takes vacation time to go on mission trips, encourages me when I'm down, and believes in me even when I don't. I love you with all of me.

CONTENTS

FOREWORD

I'm a major history buff. I love it. But here is a confession I'd be smart to deny: Almost always, my first intrigue toward some historical period or event comes from TV. As a scholar I'm ashamed to say it, but it's true; I love to watch any period piece TV show or movie I can.

Yet, one historical period I'm still waiting to see made into an HBO series is the early christological conflicts of the fourth century that arose around the Middle East and Egypt. (And truth be told, I may be waiting forever.) There are amazing stories about exiles, riots, and political engagements that surrounded the early church as it came to its understanding of who truly is this Jesus of Nazareth who was dead and now is alive.

I'm particularly a fan boy of Athanasius who, even as a young man, was led into fights with Arius and his Arians. In my fantasy HBO show, I imagine a young Athanasius played by Daniel Radcliffe.

The Arians I imagine as some cross between the villain in *The Da Vinci Code* and stormtroopers. The Arians were actually more intellectual and learned than those who would become known as the Nicene Christians. Athanasius was a young secretary to the great bishop, Alexander. Alexander opposed Arius for his claim that Jesus was not fully one with God but was made by God—and a deity, sure—but not made of the same substance and therefore not equal to God. Alexander the pastor opposed the pinheaded intellectuals—not for theoretical reasons, really, but for pastoral ones. In the experiences of his people, Bishop Alexander had seen something different. Together in worship, service, and prayer, they had experienced a living Jesus that came to them with the power to take what is dead and make it alive—and only God of sure God could do this resurrecting work.

Athanasius (again, portrayed in my mind by a young Daniel Radcliffe) stood alongside his old, loving mentor Alexander (Morgan Freeman) as the Nicene Creed was written and accepted. As Athanasius moved from secretary to Alexander's post as bishop, he would give his whole life to upholding the Nicene commitment that Jesus is sure God, begotten but not made, true God of true God. I can imagine a now-made-to-look-older Radcliffe pushing for his commitment because of his love for his mentor Alexander and his devotion to his people, even as the Arians mobilize political favors to remove him, and then Athanasius (a now out-of-shape and bearded Radcliffe) barely escapes into the darkness from the rioters who come seeking his death.

I think it would be a pretty awesome TV series! But I may be alone in that ...

Jen Bradbury has offered youth ministry something very important in this book, *The Jesus Gap*. She has waded into a conversation that has been going on for two millennia and, at least since the fourth century, has been the single distinguishing mark of these people called Christians: our understanding of who this person is, called Jesus.

Jen has so nicely laid out what young people think, drawing from both her own and others' research. And she has taken that research and offered you a truckload of practical ideas, inviting you to move your young people into a more robust Christology.

But here is the hidden gem that Jen offers in the book: In the end, it really isn't about Christology at all.

Of course, *it is.* As Athanasius and the drama of the fourth century show, it really matters what you think about Jesus. But Jen's book asserts what we often miss: In the end, the Christian faith cannot be sustained solely by the cold stone of doctrinal information. This would be as Arian and heretical as stating that Jesus is not equal with God, for Jesus is only a man. Arius made his plea in this direction because it made the most philosophical sense. But Alexander and Athanasius denied it because ultimately Christianity is not about what works intellectually but about what is experienced existentially. The pastoral always has privilege over the intellectual in the Christian faith.

So it is not Christology alone that we want our young people to know, but rather an experience, like Paul's own, of the living Christ who encounters us even today. And these experiences of the living Christ, I believe, happen today; our young people hear Jesus call to them. Alexander and Athanasius knew this because they were pastors, and we know it too if only we'd stop fetishizing knowledge and create the space for our young people to narrate their experiences and share their questions. Too often we've been too busy trying to prove a doctrine to them to stop and let them speak of how this living Jesus has been coming to them, impacting them in disturbing and exciting ways.

Jen reminds us that this is of utmost importance. We cannot, in the end, call ourselves Christians if we freeze Christianity in ideas about Jesus. Rather, like Alexander and Athanasius, we must seek the very living Jesus who comes to us.

So when Jen speaks of the "Jesus gap," she doesn't mean young people have a gap solely in their knowledge about Jesus, but something deeper. They have a gap in connecting their experience of Jesus' presence and absence in their lives with any form of reflection.

In the fourth century, confusion about Jesus was just as ramped up as it is today. But the gap we face in youth ministry is very different than it was in Athanasius' day, when most people lived with no misguided assumptions that they knew anything about Jesus. In our time, people's ignorance about Jesus is clothed in assumptions that they understand Jesus. But over and over again, Jen and the research reveal this isn't the case.

So here we stand, needing not simply to help our young people possess information about Jesus, but rather to invite them to experience the living Christ. We are asking them to take these experiences of Jesus' presence and absence in their lives and reflect on them through Scripture and church tradition—not in order to know information, but to give testimony to the depth of their experience. And this, in my mind, is the gap—the gap between young people's experience of the living Jesus and their ability to give coherent and thoughtful reflection upon it. If we can help them do this kind of reflection, it might transform their lives and be a rich blessing to the church.

Reading Jen's book will prove helpful to bridging this gap. It will make you think; and most importantly, it will move you into the depth of ministry where the living Jesus is always present, taking what is dead and bringing it back to life.

Andrew Root, PhD
Olson Baalson Professor of Youth and Family Ministry at
Luther Seminary and author of *Bonhoeffer as Youth Worker*
and *Revisiting Relational Youth Ministry*

INTRODUCTION

Less than two years into my youth ministry career, I read
Donald Miller's *Searching for God Knows What*. In this book,
Miller tells the story of teaching a class at a Bible college.
During it, he presents the gospel to his class but leaves out a
key element. He tells his students about man's sinfulness, the
depravity of culture, and how the wages of sin is death. He
shares the Good News that they can be saved from all of this
and one day experience the joy of heaven. He then asks his
students to identify the critical element of the gospel he left
out.

The result?

In Miller's words: "I presented a gospel to Christian Bible
college students and left out Jesus. Nobody noticed."[1]

At the time, this intrigued me. I remember thinking, if this is
true of Bible college students, is it also true of *my* students?

Of course, at the time, I was also pretty arrogant. I knew what
and how often I taught my teens about Jesus. So while I was
convinced this might be true for *other* youth ministries, I knew
it wasn't true of the teens involved in mine. Jesus was, after all,
at the heart of my ministry, infused in all we did.

Fast-forward seven years.

After nearly a decade in youth ministry, I'm now working
in my third congregation. I've bounced from a mainline
congregation to the evangelical world and back to a mainline
denomination. I'm also in school, pursuing a master's degree in
youth ministry. My classes have made me increasingly aware

of youth ministry research that suggests Miller's anecdote in *Searching for God Knows What* is indicative of something more widespread than I want to believe.

Consider, for a moment, the findings from two studies completed over the past decade. The National Study of Youth and Religion found today's teens are adherents of Moralistic Therapeutic Deism, a "*de facto* dominant religion" with very little to do with Jesus.[2] Another study, Fuller's College Transition Project, asked 168 youth group graduates to define what it means to be a Christian. Overall, 35 percent of the teenagers who responded "gave an answer that didn't mention Jesus."[3]

With information like this beginning to shape my perception of what teens believe about Jesus, I was eager to take a christological foundations class with author, professor, and global expert, David Livermore. As its name suggests, this class explored Christology, the branch of theology dealing with the nature, person, and deeds of Jesus. The final project for this class was to conduct a small research study on our own youth ministries in order to determine what teens believed about Jesus.

My results floored me.

Based on what I knew I'd spent the previous three and a half years teaching my youth group about Jesus, I assumed they'd know at least the basics of our Christian faith.

They didn't.

By and large, they didn't even know Jesus was God, let alone that he was sinless, or that our Christian faith is entirely dependent on him. To my horror, they also didn't understand what Jesus' crucifixion had to do with our sins.

My findings from this small study revealed a very large gap between what I thought I'd taught my youth about Jesus and what they actually knew and believed about him.

As a Christian, this Jesus gap deeply saddened me.

As a youth worker, this Jesus gap greatly alarmed me.

It propelled me to want to learn more, to see if what I'd found was limited to my youth group or if it was more widespread.

My exposure to other research made me hypothesize the latter was true—that this phenomenon was not unique to my youth ministry. Yet, because these other studies focused on the religiosity of teenagers (their piety and religious devotion) and not specifically on their Christologies (their beliefs about Jesus), I couldn't know this for sure.

So I decided to find out.

My growing interest in this subject area compelled me to study the Christology of high school teens for my culmination research project. During this yearlong study, I surveyed 369 teenagers from 16 different states who were active in their congregations' youth ministries. I also visited four representative congregations of various sizes located all across the country, from the Rocky Mountains to the East Coast. Because of my context, all congregations were part of the Evangelical Lutheran Church of America (ELCA). They included congregations in the Bible Belt, suburbs, small towns, and rural America. Not all congregations had full-time youth workers.

At each congregation I visited, I observed a program to see firsthand how, if at all, Jesus was being taught. I then interviewed adolescents, their parents, pastors, and youth workers about their beliefs in Jesus.

After doing so, I analyzed the results from both the surveys and interviews in order to answer the question, *"What's the nature of the christological understanding of high school youth in the Evangelical Lutheran Church of America (ELCA)?"*

A NOTE TO EVANGELICALS

I know it's tempting to see a modest sample size located within a particular context that's not yours and disregard its findings as irrelevant. I urge you not to do that.

These findings *are* relevant to you. I know because I, too, am an evangelical.

In college, I was part of an evangelical campus ministry that profoundly shaped my faith and theology. I learned how to do youth ministry at a Bible church. I served as the youth pastor at a multisite, multiethnic, nondenominational church for five years. In graduate school, I further developed my philosophy of ministry at the feet of some of the most prominent and widely respected youth workers in the evangelical world. I know your doctrine, your beliefs, and your churches. And what I appreciate most about you *is* your love for Jesus.

Even so, the major research studies on teens and religion suggest mainline teens aren't the only ones who struggle with their beliefs in Jesus. Yours do too. There's likely a gap— every bit as real as the one I found in the ELCA—between what you think you've taught your teens about Jesus and what they actually know and believe. This was certainly true of the nondenominational church where I was a youth pastor.

A NOTE TO MAINLINERS

I know it's equally tempting for you to see this study's focus and disregard it. Once again, I urge you not to.

These findings *are* relevant to you. I know because I, too, am a mainliner.

I grew up in a Methodist church that formed my faith. I've also spent more than half my career working for mainline churches. You have both challenged and anchored my theology. I know your doctrine, your beliefs, and your churches. What I appreciate most about you is your emphasis on grace.

That said, I know all the "Jesus talk" from evangelicals makes you nervous. I know you fear it gives Christianity a bad reputation, one that makes people label it "hypocritical" or "intolerant." But, like it or not, the foundation of our faith is Jesus of Nazareth, and my research shows our teenagers don't know him.

WHY IT MATTERS

To be clear, my research is not the end-all, be-all on this subject. No single study ever is. However, it *is* important. It gets to the heart of our faith and helps explain what teenagers actually believe about Jesus, something most other studies have only alluded to.

The truth is, what teens know about Jesus isn't much. Their Christologies are, in a word, poor.

And that's a problem not just for the evangelical or mainline world, but for the church as whole.

After all, the Christian faith is rooted in Christ. As theologian

Carl Braaten has said, the faith "stands or falls with what it knows about Jesus of Nazareth."[4]

Regardless of your denominational affiliation, I invite you to join me as we explore what teenagers believe about Jesus and what has contributed to their beliefs. Think of this book as a case study that will show you those things. As you read, search the pages for your teens. Even though the youth groups I studied weren't mine, I often found my own youth—from both evangelical and mainline congregations—there. I'm quite confident you'll find yours reflected in these pages as well.

The pages that follow are divided into three sections. In the first (**Who Is Jesus?**), you'll meet the Jesus teens believe in. The second section (**Keys for Strengthening the Christology of Teens**) will explore three of the major takeaways from this study. In the third and final section (**What's the Point?**), we'll wrestle with what the consequences of a church without Jesus are.

Throughout it all, I'll inundate you with data from my research and stories from my journey in ministry. I'll also challenge you to make changes to your ministry that in light of this research, I believe will strengthen your teens' Christologies. My hope and prayer is that stronger Christologies will, in turn, profoundly impact our congregations, the church as a whole, and the world around us.

NOTES

1. Donald Miller, *Searching for God Knows What* (Nashville: Thomas Nelson, 2004), 159.

2. Christian Smith and Melinda Lundquist Denton, *Soul Searching: The Religious and Spiritual Lives of American Teenagers* (New York: Oxford University Press, 2005), 162.

3. Kara Powell, Brad M. Griffin, and Cheryl A. Crawford, *Sticky Faith, Youth Worker Edition: Practical Ideas to Nurture Long-Term Faith in Teenagers* (Grand Rapids, MI: Zondervan/Youth Specialties, 2011), 29.

4. Carl E. Braaten, *Who Is Jesus? Disputed Questions and Answers* (Grand Rapids, MI: William B. Eerdmans Publishing Co., 2011), 5.

SECTION 1

WHO IS JESUS?

CHAPTER 1

THE JESUS TEENS BELIEVE IN

From kindergarten through my senior year in high school, every school day included a religion class. Through these classes, along with my Sunday school experience in my own church, I learned early on that Jesus is critical to the Christian faith.

Even with all of these religion classes, if you'd asked me as a child to describe Jesus, I would have said he was nice—an expected answer given the picture of Jesus I looked at for 13 years.

I'm sure you've seen it.

It's Warner Sallman's *Head of Christ* (1941), which I like to call "Swedish Jesus."[1] In it, Jesus is looking off to the right. He's wearing a white cloak. He's white, with perfect skin and long, flowing, wavy brown hair. The way the light hits him makes him appear otherworldly. He looks peaceful and serene, incapable of ever getting angry or truthfully, doing anything at all.

My image of Nice Jesus was shattered my sophomore year in high school when, during a school-wide church service, a visiting group unveiled a cross. Unlike the crosses I'd traditionally seen, this one wasn't empty. Jesus was still on it. And he no longer looked perfect. He was badly beaten with blood dripping from every possible orifice. Rather than looking serene, his face—which I still vividly remember nearly 20 years later—was pain-ridden, his mouth frozen in a perpetual grimace.

Though neither Nice Jesus nor Bloody Jesus is a complete picture of him, both greatly contributed to my understanding of who Jesus is. Nice Jesus showed me God's love: His kindness and gentleness taught me he wasn't something to be feared. Bloody Jesus turned the abstract notion that Jesus died for my sins into something concrete. Before meeting him, I couldn't understand the extent of Jesus' sacrifice for me. After meeting him, I could hardly forget it. From that day forward, whenever someone talked of Jesus, I pictured Bloody Jesus. His blood was a constant reminder of my sin and my need for a Savior.

Just as Nice Jesus and Bloody Jesus profoundly impacted my adolescent understanding of Jesus, how teens picture Jesus reflects and shapes their understanding of him as well. The truth is, for many high school teens today, Jesus is a very one-dimensional character.

WHAT THE JESUS OUR TEENS BELIEVE IN LOOKS LIKE

Consider, first of all, how teens picture Jesus. At some of my focus groups, I asked teens: *What does Jesus look like?* Some of the descriptions of Jesus were:

- He is a "white male."
- He has a "holy face."
- He has brown hair that's "long and wavy."
- He has a beard. ("It's the only way we've ever seen him.")
- He has brown eyes.
- He has a "perfectly symmetrical face—one eye is not bigger than the other."
- He wore "a white robe" and sandals.
- He is "a little dirty because he's been in the sand."
- He "had a glow that followed him."
- He is "young and healthy."

- He is strong. ("He could do anything. He could help people lift things they can't lift.")
- He is "perfect in body, perfect in strength."

Even the teenagers' parents said Jesus was a "young white male" who's "skinny."

For the most part, this picture of Jesus matches the 1940s representation of him I described earlier. It also mirrors us. For example, white teens describe Jesus as white, even though some admit knowing that "historically, he would have technically been Middle Eastern."

Jesus was "just like the average Afghani person; but if I'm thinking of him in a time of trouble, I see the Jesus I want to see: a white male about mid-20s with a beard, long hair, and a white robe."

What this young person confessed reflects a phenomenon New Testament scholar and professor Scot McKnight has observed in many of his classes. He wrote on it for *Christianity Today* in 2010, saying: "We all think Jesus is like us. Introverts think Jesus is introverted, for example, and extroverts think Jesus is extroverted. To one degree or another, we all conform Jesus to our own image."[2]

ARCHETYPES OF JESUS

To further understand the Jesus teens believe in, when I surveyed teens, I asked them the quintessential question of our faith. It's the one Jesus asks Peter in Matthew 16:15 after hearing Peter recount a litany of how other people saw him.

"Who do you say I am?"

Our faith rests on our answer to this question on the survey, which I specifically asked as a short-answer question in order to give young people the freedom to respond without any sort of constraint placed upon them. I then analyzed their responses in several ways, one of which was to group similar responses under a descriptive heading that depicts Jesus as an archetype, a pattern of thought or image that's universally present. As with any classification, these archetypes are not all-encompassing. Each one generally portrays only one facet of Jesus' character. Even though the archetypes may at times seem fanciful, none are fiction. All contain at least some attributes of Jesus found in Scripture.

SUPERHERO JESUS

From 2012 to 2014, 19 superhero movies were released. No wonder more teens' descriptions of Jesus fall into this category than any other. Young people describe Superhero Jesus in the same way they do Spider-Man: "Amazing."

Like all superheroes, Superhero Jesus is otherworldly, having been sent to our world to save it from destruction. He benefits humankind by courageously fighting his nemesis, Satan, and in the process, freeing the world from darkness. Superhero Jesus has supernatural powers including superhuman strength and invisibility, which bring him fame and notoriety. Though Superhero Jesus is willing to sacrifice himself to redeem the world, death cannot defeat him. Ultimately, he emerges victorious.

MR. ROGERS JESUS

The second largest archetype I found in my research is Mr. Rogers Jesus. This Jesus—not all that different from Nice Jesus, to whom I was introduced as a child—is a kind teacher who models the good behavior he desires from his followers. Such behavior includes acceptance, devotion, generosity, honesty, love, truthfulness, selflessness, and respect. He's someone incredibly nice who constantly does good. He's one-dimensional, never struggling with anger or any complex emotions.

In fact, in another part of the survey, the youth were given a series of word pairs and asked to choose the one from each pair that best described Jesus. While 89 percent of the adolescents described Jesus as calm, only 5 percent described him as angry. When combined, Jesus' niceness plus his calmness makes him downright wimpy.

GODLIKE JESUS

The third largest archetype of Jesus is Godlike Jesus. Godlike Jesus was conceived by the Holy Spirit and is capable of performing miracles. He's a higher power described by various "God" language including the personification of God, the Son of God, the Son of Man, and the Spirit of God. He is godlike, but not necessarily God himself.

SPIRITUAL GURU JESUS

The next largest archetype present in my research is Spiritual Guru Jesus. Spiritual Guru Jesus is not God himself, but rather someone who has a special relationship with God and can, therefore, serve as a bridge between humans and God. Spiritual Guru Jesus believes in God and has the ability and authority to forgive sins, in much the same way pastors in various traditions do. Like pastors, Spiritual Guru Jesus' job is to spread God's Word.

JOE JESUS

Another archetype found in my research is Joe Jesus. This Jesus is the guy next door; he's an everyman. In fact, it's this archetype that most directly deals with Jesus' humanness. Joe Jesus is a physical man who was a Jerusalem resident and the son of Mary. He's realistic, relatable, and a friend.

Joe Jesus was also reflected in young people's responses to the word pairs found on the survey. The youth were evenly divided in their responses to one of those word pairs. Though 47 percent of young people surveyed thought Jesus was obedient, 46 percent thought he was rebellious. In another word pair, 57 percent described Jesus as talkative, while 32 percent described him as quiet. That these adolescents were so divided in their responses to the questions suggests they see Jesus in a very human way. Perhaps more than anything else, such an even division also supports the conclusion of McKnight's *Christianity Today* article, which was that we all conform Jesus to our own image.[3]

One final place Joe Jesus appeared in my research was in my conversations with young people. One youth described him as the "average Joe." Another as "a normal person." According to another: "He's everyone. You can't really distinguish who he is. In every person's eyes he can look different."

KING JESUS

Another archetype found in my research is King Jesus. He is the Lord of Lords and the Prince of Peace. He is, in every way, a leader who rules by power.

LESS FREQUENTLY CITED ARCHETYPES

Other, less frequently cited archetypes found in my research include Martyr Jesus. This Jesus is a revolutionary Messiah who was crucified. Academic Jesus is brilliant and wise. Alien Jesus is not human. Hipster Jesus is cool. CEO Jesus is the founder of Christianity. Artist Jesus is passionately creative.

Tour Guide Jesus shows us the way.

HISTORICAL JESUS

To varying degrees, I found each of these archetypes present in the way youth workers, pastors, and parents described Jesus. Additionally, one other familiar archetype—that of Historical Jesus—was evident with the adults but wasn't evident in the answers from teenagers. This view of Jesus is prominent in the writings of people like Marcus Borg, who divides Jesus into two different entities: the Pre- and Post-Easter Jesus. Pre-Easter Jesus refers to Historical Jesus: a "Galilean Jewish peasant of the first century" who (in Borg's words) is "dead and gone."[4] In contrast, Post-Easter Jesus refers to the person his followers "continued to experience after his death as a living, spiritual, and ultimately divine reality."[5] According to Borg, though Jesus eventually became God, he was never both fully human and fully God.

Though most Christians view this understanding of Jesus as an incomplete archetype, I did encounter it in one pastor I interviewed. He intentionally distinguished between Jesus the human and Jesus the Christ, saying the latter was "the official crowning of the divinity." According to him, Jesus was an ordinary human until he became the Christ at his crucifixion, something this pastor argued was "more realistic to us than a divinity story that says he was this miraculous baby, as though he could walk and talk from birth."

ORTHODOX JESUS

Even though the archetypes of Jesus found in my research all contain attributes of the Jesus found in Scripture, none accurately represent the entire Orthodox Jesus.

Orthodox Jesus is not only godlike, but God himself. According to Jesus, "The Father and I are one" (John 10:30). At the same time, Orthodox Jesus is fully human. He was born of a woman (Galatians 4:4). Luke 8:23 tells us he slept. During his time on earth, he experienced the full range of human emotions, as evidenced in stories throughout the Gospels. He flipped over temple tables in anger (Matthew 21:12). And, according to John 11:35, he even wept.

During the three years of his public ministry, Jesus performed many miracles and—like God himself—he had the authority to forgive sins (Matthew 9:6). He also taught, according to Matthew 7:29, as "one who had authority." What's more, he called and equipped his followers to participate in God's kingdom work here and now.

Eventually, he died a physical death, after which he rose from the dead. And through that death and resurrection, he conquered death and Satan. He is now the foundation on which all of Christianity is based. Through him and only him, we receive the gift of eternal life (Romans 6:23).

THE REAL JESUS

As a teenager, encountering Bloody Jesus forever changed how I saw Jesus. Unfortunately, because Bloody Jesus contradicted so much with Nice Jesus—in whom I'd previously believed—I couldn't hold the two in tandem. Rather than expanding my view of Jesus to a more complete one, my answer to Jesus' important question ("Who do you say I am?") simply changed from one incomplete image to another. Unless we're careful, I fear the same will be true of our teens today. We'll simply replace one incomplete or false archetype of Jesus for another.

I know that's not what I want for my teens.

I'm guessing it's not what you want either.

Instead, I want our young people, like Peter in Matthew 16:16, to be able to confidently say to Jesus, "You are the Messiah, the Son of the living God."

For that to happen, teens must know and understand the real, multidimensional, Orthodox Jesus found in the pages of Scripture.

CHAPTER NOTES

1. The Warner Sallman Collection, *Head of Christ* (1941), www.warnersallman.com/collection/images/head-of-christ/.
2. Scot McKnight, "The Jesus We'll Never Know: Why Scholarly Attempts to Discover the 'Real' Jesus Have Failed. And Why That's a Good Thing," *Christianity Today*, April 9, 2010, www.christianitytoday.com/ct/2010/april/15.22.html.
3. Ibid.
4. Marcus Borg and N. T. Wright, *The Meaning of Jesus: Two Visions* (New York: HarperOne, 2007), 7.
5. Ibid.

CHAPTER 2

JESUS: NOT GOD, NOT HUMAN

What do you remember about the biology class you took in high school?

If you're anything like me, I'm guessing not much.

Despite taking both Honors Biology and Advanced Placement Biology in high school, the reality is that what I still remember from those classes can be summed up by this statement: We get half of our DNA from our moms and half of it from our dads. Even though most of our teenagers have taken biology far more recently, that's often the only part they remember too.

Believe it or not, this basic scientific fact impacts the religious beliefs of teens.

Teens, who know they're comprised of DNA from two people, assume Jesus was too. Based on the basics of biology, they conclude Jesus received 50 percent of his DNA from his dad— God—and 50 percent from his mom, a human. According to some teens, Jesus is, therefore, half and half—half God and half human—rather than fully God and fully human as orthodox Christianity asserts.

As it turns out, biology isn't the only class that influences students' beliefs about Jesus. So, too, do their English classes and—in particular—their study of Greek mythology. Familiar with the language of Greek mythology, many teens use it to describe Jesus. They conclude Jesus is like a Greek demigod. The problem is *demigod* actually implies a hierarchical relationship with someone rather than an equal standing with them. As a result, teens assume Jesus is less than God, not equal to him. According to one such teen: "God used Jesus to make believers, but God is still higher [than Jesus]."

At first, such beliefs might be easy or at least tempting to brush off. Surely such beliefs represent a minority of young people, not a majority. Maybe such beliefs are limited to specific denominations and not widespread throughout American Christianity. Or perhaps such beliefs don't actually have much of an impact on the faith of teens.

But consider the ramifications of believing Jesus is a demigod or merely half God and half human. If Jesus isn't God, then do his life and teachings matter any more than those of other people? If he isn't fully God, then how could Jesus have performed miracles? How could he have risen from the dead? On the flip side, if Jesus isn't fully human, then how can God relate to us? How can we relate to God? If Jesus isn't fully human, then is a relationship with an almighty God even possible?

In the words of theologian Carl Braaten:

> If Jesus were merely a man, he would share the predicament of all human beings. He would himself need to be saved; he could not be the Savior ... Likewise, if Jesus were only God ... and not fully human, he would have no point of contact with those who need to be saved.[1]

As you can see, what we believe about both Jesus' divinity and his humanity matters greatly. No wonder the apostle Paul declares Jesus to be the church's "chief cornerstone" (Ephesians 2:20).

WHAT TEENS BELIEVE ABOUT JESUS' DIVINITY AND HUMANITY

With stakes as high as these, it's critically important for us to know what teens actually believe about Jesus' divinity and humanity. Without first knowing this, how can we possibly hope to instill in them the basics of our Christian faith?

To investigate this, my survey asked youth: *Is Jesus God?* And they were evenly divided in their answers to this question: 44 percent answered yes; 44 percent said no; 12 percent confessed, "I don't know." (See Figure 1.)

This means even though orthodox Christianity is built on the premise that Jesus *is* God, more than half (56 percent) of the adolescents I surveyed either did not believe or did not know Jesus was God. Given that those I surveyed were all active in their churches' youth ministries, this finding is striking.

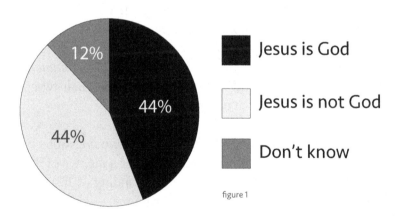

figure 1

Truthfully, I wish I could say this problem was unique to one denomination. However, other research suggests it's not. According to Robert Wuthnow's 2003 Religion and Diversity Survey, "About two-thirds of young and old alike regarded Jesus as the divine Son of God."[2] This, of course, means about one-third of young and old alike *don't* regard Jesus as the divine Son of God. Additionally, in a survey of 877 adolescents conducted in 2010 at Reach Workcamps, researcher Mike Nappa found that 41 percent of surveyed adolescents either didn't know or didn't believe Jesus is God.[3]

For the students I spoke with, one of the stumbling blocks to believing Jesus is God is his humanity. According to one, "God's a god and [Jesus] is a human." Another suggested that instead of being God, Jesus was "just very influenced by God."

Based on these responses, it's not surprising that young people had an easier time affirming Jesus' humanity than they did his divinity. More than half of the teenagers I surveyed (54 percent) believed Jesus was fully human, while 31 percent said he wasn't, and 15 percent admitted they didn't know.

Now, the reality is, as Christians we hold these two seemingly contradictory statements in tension, believing both to be true: Jesus is fully God while, at the same time, he is also fully human. As a result, I cared not just about how young people answered the questions *Is Jesus God?* and *Was Jesus human?* independently of one another, but also about how their two answers compared to each other.

So I looked at adolescents' answers to these two questions side by side. Doing so revealed that just over a quarter of them (26 percent) affirmed the orthodox understanding of Jesus— believing he is both fully God and fully human—while 23 percent believed Jesus is just another human, and 12 percent believed Jesus is God alone. Interestingly, 17 percent of the young people rejected Jesus as both God and human.

For me, it's that last statistic that's most interesting. If teens don't believe Jesus is God and they don't believe he's human, then who exactly do they think he is?

To find out, I turned again to teenagers' responses to one of the short-answer questions I asked on the survey: *Who is Jesus?* In addition to analyzing this question by grouping similar responses under the descriptive headings that depicted Jesus as the archetypes you saw in chapter 1, I also analyzed their responses to this question in order to determine how many said the same thing.

The most common response to this question was that Jesus was the "Son of God." (See Figure 2.) In fact, 62 percent of young people described Jesus this way. They also commonly called Jesus their "Savior," someone who "died for us," someone who God "sent" into the world, and a "human" or "man."

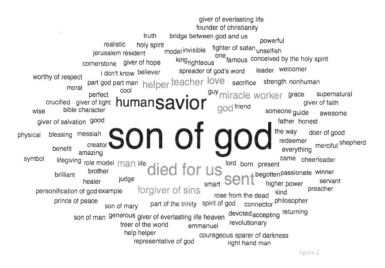

figure 2

While there's certainly value in hearing teens describe Jesus in their own words, in this particular case, what I was most interested in was how those who said Jesus was neither God nor human answered this particular question. Isolating their responses revealed that 83 percent of this subgroup described Jesus as the "Son of God." Given this, what does that phrase "Son of God" actually mean to teens? In their minds, is being the Son of God the same thing as being God himself?

When I asked young people these questions, their responses were mixed. Some agreed these two things were the same. According to one of them, Jesus is "fully God but he's still the Son of God."

Others were less certain. Many agreed being the Son of God wasn't the same thing as being God. However, most who said this couldn't articulate why this was. Instead, they kept repeating, "Jesus was human."

Still others reverted to logic similar to those who described Jesus as a demigod. In our culture, *son* is a word that defines you in relationship with someone else. It automatically implies you're less than, or from a biological standpoint, no longer "fully" the person you originated from. Thus, many young people in the study who believed Jesus was the Son of God didn't necessarily believe he was God himself. To them, the phrase "Son of God" was almost otherworldly, referring to someone who was neither God, nor human, but a unique third category.

STOP TALKING ABOUT GOD

As youth workers, our job is not to create a thriving youth ministry that will ensure the continuation of our congregations; it's to create followers of Jesus. If the majority of our youth don't believe or don't know Jesus is God, then we're failing at our primary calling as youth workers.

The good news is we don't have to continue failing. Instead, there are practical ways through which we can help young people understand the difficult reality that Jesus is both simultaneously God and human.
To begin, don't just talk about God. Instead, talk specifically about Jesus.

Now, before you say, "I already do!" consider this. During my visits to various congregations, I asked youth workers: *How frequently do you talk about Jesus and not just God in your youth ministry?*

Inevitably, youth workers would enthusiastically respond, "All the time."

Then I'd attend their youth ministry program. When I did, do you know what I heard?

Generic God-talk, not Jesus-talk.

Often this phenomenon wasn't limited to just youth ministry gatherings; it was also prevalent in the larger communities of faith.

At one congregation I visited, I attended the church's Sunday morning worship service. During the service, the senior pastor preached on John 6:25-59, the passage in which Jesus declares himself to be the Bread of Life. While I lost track of how many times this pastor referred to God in his sermon, I can tell you exactly how many times he said the name of Jesus—aside from reading the word *Jesus* in the passage itself: *none.* Instead of talking about Jesus, this pastor took a Gospel story that was unequivocally *about* Jesus and made it about God.

Regrettably, I can't tell you exactly why this was. What I can tell you is that after observing this phenomenon in multiple congregations, I finally asked a youth worker about it. Michelle, one of the youth workers I interviewed, said, "Talking frankly about Jesus can make kids uncomfortable. It's perceived as preachy. So it becomes really easy to talk vaguely about God and faith."

As Michelle said, talking vaguely about God is easy. I'd even argue it's safer than talking about Jesus. God is ambiguous enough that people can interpret him as they please. One person's God may differ from that of the person sitting next to them.

Not so with Jesus. Jesus is specific. He's an actual person who said and did certain things that not everyone likes or agrees with. When we talk about Jesus, we therefore run the risk of offending and excluding people. Knowing this, we sometimes retreat, willingly settling for God instead of Jesus. If that's the case for church workers, then how much scarier must it be for adolescents to talk specifically about Jesus?

No wonder their responses mirrored those of their youth workers. When I asked teenagers how frequently they talked about Jesus in their youth ministries, like their youth workers, they enthusiastically said, "All the time." However, when I observed them in their youth ministries, that's not what I heard. Often the teenagers would start off talking about Jesus, but before long, their language would shift from Jesus-talk to generic God-talk.

The truth is God-talk simply does not impact the Christian faith formation of young people in the same way that Jesus-talk does. According to Kenda Creasy Dean in *Almost Christian*, "Conversational Christianity requires Jesus-talk, not just God-talk ... Jesus is simply not an optional category for Christians."[4]

DON'T JUST TALK ABOUT JESUS OCCASIONALLY

In order to help our youth understand that Jesus is both fully God and fully human, not only do we need to talk specifically about Jesus, but we also need to do so every single time our youth ministries gather.

While this might seem like Youth Ministry 101 to you, there are people in our congregations for whom this idea is revolutionary. What's more, there are also people in our congregations who are actually opposed to this.

For example, every once in a while I meet with youth group dropouts or their parents to find out how our youth ministry can better connect with families like theirs. On one such occasion, I met with a mom over coffee and asked why she thought our youth ministry had failed to connect with her son.

This concerned mother—an active member of my congregation—told me she believed it was because we talked about Jesus too much. According to her, youth group needed to be more fun and less churchy so we could effectively reach teens like her son, who simply weren't interested in Jesus. To do that, the focus of our time together needed to be games. We could talk about Jesus, but only as an afterthought, as an aside to a great night of fun.

Though it was honest, this mom's response was disheartening. Unfortunately, I know she's not the only person in my congregation who believes fun and Jesus don't mix. What's more, I guarantee there are people like this concerned mom in your congregation as well. So what do we do?

First, let me tell you what we *can't* do: continue to ignore Jesus or even settle for talking about God instead. Clearly, that's not working.

As an alternative, dare I suggest we show the naysayers another way?

Instead of just replacing Jesus-talk with God-talk, fearlessly talk specifically about Jesus every single time you meet. Then watch as he transforms the lives of the youth you're privileged to serve. Transformed lives will silence your critics in a way that nothing else will.

So try it. Talk about Jesus every time you meet, even though doing so will inevitably mean you talk less about God. That's okay since Jesus is the foundation of our faith. As Paul says in 1 Corinthians 3:11, "For no one can lay any foundation other than the one already laid, which is Jesus Christ." Jesus, not God, is what differentiates our Christian faith from every other religion in the world.

As youth workers, this means we cannot actually talk about Jesus too much. No matter what concerned parents or volunteers might tell us, we cannot overdo Jesus. If our teens leave our ministries with Jesus as the foundation of their faith, we have done our jobs well.

Likewise, don't be afraid to talk about Jesus more than you talk about the Holy Spirit. This is especially important when you take into account the brain development of teens. Younger teens—in particular, those in junior high as well as underclassmen in high school—still think in concrete ways. That's why both God and the Holy Spirit are so difficult for younger teens to understand. Those parts of the Trinity cannot be seen, touched, or felt.

In contrast, Jesus is concrete. We have detailed records of who he was, where he lived, who his friends were, what he taught, and what he did. For this reason, we can easily picture him. In so doing, Jesus becomes the manifestation of God to young people. His humanity is what enables them to relate to and know God intimately.

Now, even though I believe we should unashamedly talk about Jesus more than we talk about any other person of the Trinity, please don't misunderstand me. I'm not actually suggesting we only preach from the Gospels (though I think there are worse things we could do). Instead, consider the words of Martin Luther, "The Bible is the cradle wherein Christ is laid." If that's true, then everything in Scripture points to Jesus. Our job as youth workers is to help our young people connect the dots.

To do this, teach through the Bible. Start in Genesis and end in Revelation. Within a year, cover the basic story arc of the Bible without feeling the need to address every chapter within it. As you do, help teens put the pieces of the Scripture puzzle together not just chronologically, but theologically. Help them see Jesus as a beloved and innocent son in the story of Abraham almost sacrificing Isaac; in Moses as the liberator of God's people; in the Passover meal as the lamb; in various judges and kings of Israel as our promised leader; and even in the story of Job as redeemer. Identify the themes found throughout Scripture—the ones that point to the fulfillment of God's plan for the redemption of the world—and then explain how Jesus *is* the fulfillment of that plan.

When you reach the Gospels, explore passages that showcase both Jesus' divinity and his humanity. Bask in the wonder of the miracles that leave no doubt Jesus is God. Then turn to the stories of Jesus sleeping, eating, and weeping—doing the very things all humans do. Challenge teens to wrestle with the moments in which Jesus appears to be more godlike than humanlike or vice versa. Ask: *To do miracles, did Jesus have to forsake his humanity? In order to sleep, did Jesus have to stop being God, even for a moment?* Give teens the freedom and the space in which to honestly wrestle with these questions, trusting that Jesus himself will meet them in the midst of their doubts and uncertainties.

EXPLAIN CHRISTIANESE

During college, I studied abroad in Russia. Doing so meant learning the basics of not only an entirely new language, but also an entirely different alphabet.

While I was there, some American friends visited me. Since I was used to the Cyrillic alphabet at that point, I took my friends on a tour of Moscow, easily using public transit to do so. As we got off the subway once, I pointed to the exit sign, written in Cyrillic, and said, "That way."

In frustration, my friend exclaimed, "If I could just recognize the letters, it'd sure be a lot easier for me to get around here!"

I sometimes wonder how often teens feel like that in church. Is our Christianese so foreign to them that they think, *If I could just understand these words, this faith thing would sure be easier for me to figure out?*

Given where teens are in their cognitive development, still transitioning from concrete to abstract thought, clarity is especially important as it pertains to fostering their foundational beliefs in Jesus. As you explore the Jesus story, take time to explain confusing Christianese words (like *grace*) to teens.

Consider for a moment how one of the youth workers I interviewed responded to the question: *What are your foundational beliefs about Jesus?*

> God had decided we needed someone to help us connect with God, so he gave us Jesus. He was the person who gave us the gift of grace. No matter how we are as human beings or how many mistakes we make, we still are going to go to heaven. We're still going to be with God.

Notice this youth worker's use of the word *grace*. Obviously, this word means something significant to him. Yet, for the person listening to his response, his use of the word *grace* is ambiguous and perhaps even confusing.

As youth workers, we need to be extremely aware of how and when we use Christianese words like *grace*. To better help teens understand abstract theological concepts, rather than repeating them again and again without explanation, try utilizing concrete metaphors.

Recently, I challenged my adult leaders to come up with concrete metaphors to explain grace, and this was the result:

"Grace is like a snow day."
"Grace is like paying it forward."
"Grace is like an Etch A Sketch: When you mess up, you get a do-over."

Even though these metaphors will all eventually break down, they still help make an abstract reality concrete and, therefore, more understandable for teens. That said, reread those metaphors. Do you notice what's missing?

Jesus.

If we lose Jesus in the process of translating an abstract truth into a concrete reality, that concrete reality does us no good. Thus, we have to take metaphors one step further and explicitly connect the dots—all the way back to Jesus.

DISSECT ABSTRACT LANGUAGE

In the same way we need to translate Christianese into language that makes sense to teens, we also need to break down abstract language we encounter in Scripture.

Consider, for example, Jesus' teaching on the wide and narrow gates in Matthew 7:13-14.

Enter through the narrow gate. For wide is the gate
and broad is the road that leads to destruction, and
many enter through it. But small is the gate and
narrow the road that leads to life, and only a few
find it.

At first glance, you might wonder why I'd include this example
here. Gates are, after all, concrete—easy for us to visualize.
Yet, in this passage, gates are used in a rather abstract way.
Imagine, then, the challenge of discussing this passage with
junior high students, who might well assume that if a gate were
narrow, fat people wouldn't be able to pass through it. As youth
workers, we have to be prepared for and ready to address such
assumptions before we can begin wrestling with the theological
truths found in passages like these.

As another example, think about the phrase "Son of God,"
which is how more than three-quarters of the young people
who said Jesus was neither God nor human referred to him.

Knowing this, when you encounter this phrase in Scripture,
dissect it. Walk alongside your group as you investigate stories
that specifically refer to Jesus as God's Son, like that of Jesus'
baptism in Matthew 3:13-17. Rather than ignoring phrases like
"Son of God" in the text or assuming teens interpret them like
you do, ask:

- *What do you think it means for Jesus to be God's Son?*
- *If Jesus is God's Son, is he still fully God?*
- *Does the fact that Jesus is God's Son mean he's
  somehow less than God?*

This is especially important because of the church's inclusion
of phrases like "Son of God" in the creeds. To be clear, I
know that not all congregations regularly recite creeds in
worship. Even so, I'd bet that if you dig deep enough into your

congregation's statement of beliefs, it would either reference a creed or borrow language from it.

Here's why this is important. Remember how more than half of the total adolescents I surveyed described Jesus as the "Son of God" in their response to the short-answer question: *Who is Jesus?*

Well, this phrase, "Son of God," is creedal language. It appears in both the Apostles' Creed (which states Jesus is "God's only Son") and in the Nicene Creed (which calls Jesus "the only Son of God").

In addition to "Son of God," many of the other titles young people gave Jesus including "Lord" and "judge" are also ones given to him in the creeds. According to the Apostles' Creed, Jesus is "our Lord." Likewise, the Nicene Creed calls him "one Lord." Similarly, the Apostles' Creed acknowledges that Jesus "will come to judge the living and the dead." So, too, does its equivalent in the Nicene Creed: "He will come again in glory to judge the living and the dead."

In actuality, 73 percent of the language used by adolescents to answer my question is found in the creeds. That so many of their responses came from the creeds suggests even language we don't understand impacts how we talk about Jesus. Such language gives teens in our youth ministries a way to answer questions for which they otherwise have no words. In doing so, it becomes identity-giving for many of them.

This means when we invoke and expand upon creedal language, we strengthen adolescents' understanding of who Jesus is. If your congregation isn't one that explicitly uses creeds in worship, consider introducing creeds through your youth ministry. Use the creeds to discuss the question: *Who is Jesus?* Then discuss the origins of the creeds and the roles they've had in church history.

If your congregation regularly uses creeds in worship, chances are that at some point you've already taught the creeds to your teens. If that's the case, take steps to ensure you do more than just teach the creeds once and then forget about them.

As adolescents continue to grow in their ability to think abstractly, help them process what they believe about Jesus in terms of creedal language, integrating and incorporating both abstract thought and concrete terms. Encourage teens to continually wrestle with the meaning of the creeds, rather than unquestionably profess them without ever thinking about what they're saying.

Regardless of how entrenched creeds are in your congregation's DNA, challenge teens to individually or communally construct their own creed. As you walk through this process together, give teens the freedom to describe Jesus and their faith in their own words, using modern-day language. At the same time, ensure that your creed upholds both Scripture as well as tradition in its understanding of Jesus. Once written, use these creeds in worship. Invite your entire congregation to say them together as an affirmation of faith.

When I did a series on the Apostles' Creed with my youth ministry, they formulated and wrote the following creed of their own:

We believe in God, the author of life and the sustainer of all things. We believe that God's love never ends and that he guides us today and is always with us, a light in the darkness and our comfort in hard times.

We believe that out of love, God sent his only Son, Jesus, to die on the cross and rise again to forgive our sins. We believe that Jesus, who is God, also connects us to God the Father and enables us to experience a life filled with grace and mercy. We believe that Jesus now sits at the right hand of God the Father, where he is speaking to God for us.

We believe in the Holy Spirit, an invisible power in our lives that knows and guides us. Through him, we experience God in our daily lives.

We believe in one church that is the body of Christ and our home, a way for us to worship God and serve Christ with others.

Amen.

After wrestling with the wording of this creed for weeks, my congregation then recited it together one Sunday morning in worship. Hearing the body of Christ come together to speak the words of faith written by high school teens was powerful. Through this creed, our youth showed our larger congregation the vibrancy and reality of their faith in Jesus, which in turn bolstered and encouraged the faith of an older generation who worries continually about the future of the church.

At the same time, saying these words of faith together with their brothers and sisters in Christ was an act of unity and solidarity that told our young people: *In those moments when you doubt the words you've written, we'll stand with you. When you doubt that Jesus is God, we'll be here to continually remind you of this truth until you can once again proclaim it for yourself.*

Beyond that, saying these words out loud allowed teens (and perhaps some adults as well) to do what Creasy Dean calls "speak their faith into being."[5] That, in turn, gave them the opportunity to take ownership of what they believe not just about faith in general, but specifically about Jesus.

IT'S NOT ABOUT PASSING A TEST

When we took biology in high school, we had to know basic genetics in order to pass the test and, ultimately, the class. As we've already seen, the basic genetics that we—and our teens—learn in biology impacts our understanding of Jesus.

Even so, the truth is that understanding who Jesus is—that he is both fully God and fully human—is not about passing a test. It's about building a sturdy, lasting foundation of faith. And if the entirety of our Christian faith is built upon Jesus, then I'd argue that the integrity of the structure depends significantly on Jesus being fully God and fully human.

CHAPTER NOTES

1. Carl E. Braaten, *Who Is Jesus? Disputed Questions and Answers* (Grand Rapids, MI: William B. Eerdmans Publishing Company, 2011), 69.

2. Robert Wuthnow, *After the Baby Boomers: How Twenty- and Thirty-Somethings Are Shaping the Future of American Religion* (Princeton, NJ: Princeton University Press), 2007.

3. Mike Nappa, *The Jesus Survey: What Christian Teens Really Believe and Why* (Grand Rapids, MI: Baker Books, 2012).

4. Kenda Creasy Dean, *Almost Christian: What the Faith of Our Teenagers Is Telling the American Church* (New York: Oxford University Press, 2010), 139.

5. Ibid.

CHAPTER 3

JESUS: AN IMPERFECT HUMAN

American culture upholds perfection as an ideal. We celebrate models who have "perfect" bodies. We applaud students who get straight As. Even in the church, we applaud perfection. We celebrate those who appear to have their lives together and those who appear to be without sin (or at least without the kinds of sins we like to call out and name).

The result?

Rather than being authentic and vulnerable, we're pretending to be people we are not.

Just think for a moment about your typical Sunday morning worship gathering. When you ask someone how she's doing, what's her typical response?

"I'm good, thanks."

Chances are also good that when people ask how you're doing, you answer in a similar fashion—even if you've had a terrible week. Rather than risk showing emotion and appearing to be weak, in need of help, or anything less than perfect, we settle for an answer we know will appease everyone.

The result is catastrophic to our communities. According to Brennan Manning in *The Ragamuffin Gospel*:

> At Sunday worship, as in every dimension of our existence, many of us pretend to believe we are sinners. Consequently, all we can do is pretend we

have been forgiven. As a result, our whole spiritual life is pseudo-repentance and pseudo-bliss.[1]

The irony is that even though we seek and expect perfection from our leaders and ourselves, many people don't actually believe Jesus was perfect. According to researcher David Kinnaman, "Young adults are more likely than any other age group to believe Jesus sinned, to doubt the miracles Jesus performed, and to express skepticism about his resurrection."[2] LifeWay's Millennial Study also found that Millennials are "evenly divided on the sinlessness of Jesus."[3]

Such beliefs have profound implications for our faith.

If Jesus sinned, what makes him any different than the rest of us? After all, as much as we strive for perfection, we are still sinners. As Paul says in Romans 3:23, "All have sinned and fall short of the glory of God."

If Jesus sinned, how can he forgive our sins, something we need since Romans 6:23 tells us the wages of sin is death?

And, if Jesus sinned, how could he be an acceptable sacrifice for our sins—a spotless lamb, as the Old Testament taught that God required? If Jesus sinned, then he too would—as Mike Nappa so aptly said in his research—"need a Savior."[4]

Ultimately, if Jesus sinned, how could he be God?

WHAT TEENS BELIEVE ABOUT JESUS' PERFECTION

Aware of varying beliefs about Jesus' sinlessness (or lack thereof) from other studies—as well as the profound implications these beliefs have on our faith—I wanted to explore this issue in my own research as well. To do so, I asked young people: *Was Jesus perfect?* I chose to ask teens about Jesus' perfection because *perfect* is one of the words used in Scripture to describe God. Among other places, we see this attribute applied to God in Matthew 5:48 when Jesus commands his followers, "Be perfect, therefore, as your heavenly Father is perfect." If God is perfect and, according to orthodox Christianity, Jesus is God, then it follows that Jesus is also perfect. (Note: I realize *perfect* can mean different things to different people. In order to make sure teens interpreted the questions on my survey as I intended them, before surveying my first round of youth, I "tested" my survey on a small group of "churched" teens. Teens in this test group said that in this context, they interpreted *perfect* to mean "without sin.") When asked about Jesus' perfection, 34 percent of teens affirmed Jesus was perfect. (See Figure 3.)

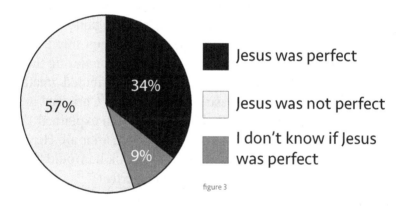

Jesus was perfect

Jesus was not perfect

I don't know if Jesus was perfect

figure 3

In order to verify people's responses to certain questions, one technique commonly employed in research is to ask the same question in multiple ways, and then compare the responses of individuals with one another. To do that here, I also asked young people: *Did Jesus sin?* Based on our definition of perfection, we'd expect the number of youth who said Jesus was perfect to be approximately the same as those who said he did not sin. Indeed, 36 percent of the youth said Jesus did not sin.

Having designed these two questions with comparison in mind, I also did a side-by-side analysis of people's responses to these two questions. Doing so revealed that 72 percent of teens remained consistent in their beliefs from one question to the next. Of that 72 percent, 28 percent said Jesus was perfect and that he had no sin; 44 percent said Jesus was imperfect and that he sinned. Seven percent contradicted themselves in some way, saying either Jesus was perfect but he sinned; or Jesus did not sin, but he still wasn't perfect.

IMPERFECT JESUS

Intrigued by how many teens believed Jesus to be imperfect or sinful, during my focus groups, I set out to determine why. To do so, I asked: *Do you think Jesus sinned?* Even though I always asked about sin, in every focus group, teens described Jesus in terms of his perfection or imperfection (again indicating the two words are interchangeable in their minds). Based on young people's responses to this question during the focus groups, one thing that appears to have contributed greatly to their confusion about this issue is the orthodox Christian understanding that Jesus is fully human. One teen explained her confusion by saying, "Jesus was God's Son, after all. He was human. It's really hard to know. You'd think he would be perfect. But humans—it's impossible to be perfect."

In addition to contributing to teens' confusion about Jesus' perfection, Jesus' humanity is also one reason why adolescents believe Jesus is imperfect. At one of the focus groups I held, none of the youth present thought Jesus was perfect. Instead, all spoke of his sin. According to one, "Jesus sinned because he was a human being like the rest of us. Even the best people in the world sin."

In truth, you can't fault that young person's logic. Jesus was human. All humans sin. Therefore, Jesus sinned. Such logic was actually widespread among those in my focus groups.

60

According to one teen, "Like every human, Jesus messed up every once in a while." Another said, "He was a child. All children make mistakes. Even if it's not written in the Bible, there's got to be something he did that wasn't 100 percent morally correct or spiritually correct, whether it was at the age of 2 or 15." Other youth readily agreed that just because Jesus' sins aren't recorded in the Bible, that doesn't mean he's sinless. According to them, the people who wrote the Bible may have left out Jesus' sins intentionally, as part of a conspiracy designed to "make Jesus more godly."

EXAMPLES OF JESUS' SINS

When asked to cite specific examples of Jesus' sin, some individuals in all four of my focus groups talked about Jesus cleansing the temple in Matthew 21:12-13. One young person explained, "Jesus went through the temple and seeing a bunch of people set up, he flipped tables and broke things. That probably wasn't necessary. He could have been peaceful and nonviolent."

My interviewees also said the Bible contained other examples of Jesus' sin. To them, Jesus staying behind at the temple when he was 12 years old was an example of disobeying his parents, breaking the Ten Commandments, and therefore, sinning. Others suggested his blatant disregard for the Jewish law was also sin. One cited Jesus' failure to honor the Sabbath as a particular example of this. This young person was, however, quick to brush this off because "the Pharisees were trying to trap [Jesus]."

Similarly, some of the youth thought Jesus sinned because he was anti-establishment. According to one, "Jesus had a tendency to disregard secular rules and things. There's this part in the Bible that says government is established by God. If he's disobeying the government, then he can't be fully perfect."

Some teens also thought Jesus lied and cheated, though none could think of specific examples of these behaviors. Strangely, though adolescents were willing to call Jesus a liar and cheater, they vehemently agreed Jesus never would have stolen anything. According to them, as God's Son, Jesus was "a somewhat good person" who would not have done such a thing.

Still other young people differentiated between Jesus' actions and his thoughts, claiming he sinned in regard to the latter but not the former. One said, "Jesus might not have physically sinned, but he thought about things. You can always sin with your thoughts."

Additional youths linked Jesus' sinful nature to grace and forgiveness. According to one, "Jesus probably sinned. He knew all along that your sins would be forgiven." Another alleged that without sin, Jesus would have had no need for God. In his words, "I think he sinned quite a bit. He talked to God a lot. You don't talk to God if you don't sin. You had to sin quite a bit in order to keep your relationship close to God."

Amidst this sea of statements about Jesus' imperfection, it's important to remember that just over a quarter (28 percent) of the young people I surveyed actually concluded Jesus was perfect. Interestingly, only the youth from the congregation I visited in the Bible Belt were able to articulate why they believed this. One said if Jesus had sinned, "He wouldn't have been a perfect sacrifice." Another elaborated, saying, "All who sin fall short of the glory of God. If you sin, you can't get into heaven. It would make no sense for Jesus to have sinned and even get into heaven, let alone be the sacrifice for all of us." According to another, "If Jesus sinned, it would have defeated the purpose of him coming. He was our example of how we should live."

THE RELATIONSHIP BETWEEN JESUS' DIVINITY AND PERFECTION

Since God is incapable of sin, what teens believe about Jesus' perfection and sinlessness also relates to what they believe about his divinity. To further explore this relationship, I compared a teen's answer to the question about Jesus' perfection with his or her answer to the question: *Is Jesus God?* (See Figure 4.) Doing so revealed that the largest percentage of the youth surveyed (29 percent) believe Jesus was an imperfect human. (Such students said Jesus was neither God, nor perfect.) In addition, 21 percent of teens adhere to the orthodox Christian understanding that Jesus is a perfect God; 20 percent think he's an imperfect God; and 10 percent believe Jesus was a perfect human.

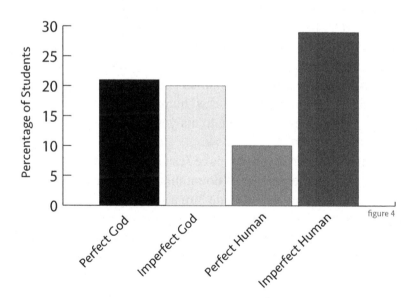

figure 4

MAKING SENSE OF YOUNG PEOPLE'S BELIEFS

So why is it that the largest percentage of youth surveyed believe Jesus was an imperfect human?

Perhaps it's because we've overemphasized Jesus' humanity.

At each congregation I visited, I asked pastors and youth workers: *When you talk about Jesus, what do you say?* Depending on their responses to this question, sometimes I'd also follow up by asking: *Which, if any, do you emphasize more: Jesus' humanity or his divinity?*

Time and time again, both pastors and youth workers talked about emphasizing Jesus' humanity. One youth worker explained he focused on Jesus' humanity because he wanted to "connect youth to Jesus' coming down here and being in flesh and being the same with us." He went on to say, "Even though he was also divine, he was a human and understands our struggles." By emphasizing Jesus' humanity, this youth worker hoped to make Jesus relatable to his youth.

Unfortunately, our desire to make Jesus relatable has come with a cost. In the process of doing this, we've turned Jesus into one of us, and we've made him a sinner, just like us. As a result, teens can easily envision hanging out with Jesus—at school, on Friday nights, and with their friends. What they can't do is relate to him as God, or believe he can make a difference in their lives, or even forgive their sins.

INVESTIGATE THE AUTHORITY OF SCRIPTURE

Without the ability to relate to Jesus as God, the faith of teens is impotent.

Thankfully, there are several things we can do to change this.

As Christians, our foundational beliefs about who Jesus is come from Scripture. The problem is, many of today's teens don't believe Scripture is trustworthy. Instead, they question its authority. They're skeptical both of what's in Scripture as well as what's not. To teens who doubt the trustworthiness of Scripture, it's entirely reasonable to believe that even if Jesus sinned, his sins weren't recorded in the Bible because its authors were part of a conspiracy to portray him in a positive light.

To address this, don't assume teenagers view Scripture the same way you do. Instead, find out what your teens actually believe about Jesus and the Bible. Then start where they're at. If they don't believe the Bible is trustworthy, teach them why you believe it is.

Since many of the questions teens have about the Bible's trustworthiness stem from their skepticism (or lack of knowledge) regarding the canonization process, openly discuss it. Talk about how we got the Bible we have today. Discuss the process of translating Scripture and the care given to that process. Assure your group that their questions will be welcomed as you wrestle with the work of the Holy Spirit in the canonization process.

Talk about the unity of the Bible. Share how even though the Bible was written over the course of a 2,000-year span, in three different languages, and by more than 40 different authors from all walks of life, all of Scripture points to Jesus. As part of this, discuss the unifying plot of Scripture, from what Scot McKnight calls "creation to consummation."[5] Help teens in your ministry learn not just how to quote individual Scripture passages, but how those passages are part of the larger story of Scripture.

Investigate and debunk popular conspiracy theories surrounding Scripture. Give teens the opportunity to read for themselves the lost books of the Bible—those books found in the Apocrypha or, better yet, those left out of Scripture entirely. Discussing them removes both their allure and mystery. At the same time, it helps teens understand why the Bible they possess is reliable.

TEACH JESUS' HUMANITY *AND* HIS DIVINITY

Once the authority of Scripture is established, it will be easier to establish Jesus' sinlessness. To do this, as we discussed in chapter 2, explore Scripture passages that showcase both Jesus' humanity *and* his divinity. When you teach Jesus' humanity, paint an accurate picture of the real Jesus, not merely the one we've created in our own image. Discuss where Jesus lived and what that suggests about his appearance. Add to or even replace images of Swedish Jesus with a Middle Eastern or African Jesus.

Be just as intentional in teaching about Jesus' divinity as you are about teaching teens about his humanity. Since our emphasis on Jesus' humanity has greatly contributed to their assumptions that he sinned, emphasizing Jesus' divinity is vital for strengthening this particular aspect of teens' Christologies.

Be creative with how you do this. Use hymn or song lyrics to prompt a discussion on Jesus' divinity. Consider, for example, the lyrics of the hymn, "What a Friend We Have in Jesus":

> *What a friend we have in Jesus,*
> *All our sins and griefs to bear!*
> *What a privilege to carry*
> *Everything to God in prayer!*
> *Oh, what peace we often forfeit,*
> *Oh, what needless pain we bear,*

All because we do not carry
Everything to God in prayer![6]

After singing this hymn, wrestle with what characteristics of Jesus make him a good friend. Then debate how he is and isn't like our other friends; how the fact that Jesus is God distinguishes him from all other people in our lives. Wrestle with how Jesus being God also enables him, as this song suggests, to bear our sins and grief.

REPLACE WWJD WITH WDJD

If you were around in the Christian subculture in the 1990s, you're no doubt familiar with the popular phrase *WWJD?* or *What Would Jesus Do?* Maybe, like me, you even sported a bracelet, T-shirt, or bumper sticker featuring this acronym.

My research suggests it's high time for this acronym to die. In order to help young people develop stronger beliefs about Jesus, let's stop speculating and instead, go back to the basics. One way to do this is to replace *WWJD?* with *WDJD?* or *What Did Jesus Do?*

To do this, teach the story of Jesus: who he was, what he did, and why he was important. Do so without worrying about being repetitive. Rick Lawrence says in *Jesus-Centered Youth Ministry*, "Many of us have been following Jesus so long that we think we already know everything there is to know about him."[7] The truth is, however, even teens who've grown up in the church don't actually know the Jesus story well.

DIG INTO JESUS' OWN WORDS

To help teens learn the Jesus story, consider your language. In our attempts to make Jesus relevant, how often do we label him a rebel or a revolutionary? While it's possible such words describe Jesus, at least to some extent, they might also contribute to the widespread belief among teens that

Jesus sinned.

After all, in today's society, rebels, revolutionaries, and radicals are people who break the rules. Thus, when we label Jesus a "rebel," young people naturally conclude he, too, broke the rules. And if he broke the rules, then he sinned.

With that in mind, one key to strengthening this aspect of teens' Christologies is to force teens to wrestle with not only the labels we give Jesus, but also the Jesus found in the Gospels. In particular, help teens examine Jesus' words. According to Lawrence, "When we help teenagers focus on the red stuff, we anchor their faith in reality, not conjecture."[8]

I once did a series in my high school youth ministry titled "Radical Jesus." During that series, we discussed the widow's mite, the story in which a poor woman gives all she has in the temple, while Jesus sits there and watches her. As I taught this, I invited my own students to come forward and give an offering.

As they did, I sat in a prominent spot and watched them. After our offering concluded, I recounted which of them gave and which did not. I then asked those who gave nothing to explain themselves.

Of course, teens in my ministry were outraged.

One youth, exclaimed, "That's not what Jesus would do! He wouldn't sit there and judge people!"

I then asked them to reread Mark 12:41, which says Jesus "sat down opposite the place where offerings were put" and watched the crowd giving to the church.

After doing so, I asked them how what I did was different than what Jesus did.

This led to a riveting discussion through which the teens learned that the Jesus found in the Gospels does not often behave the way we expect him to. He simply refuses to be boxed into a certain belief or behavioral system.

TEACH JESUS' SINLESSNESS

As you teach the Jesus story, specifically teach Jesus' sinlessness. Teach it in terms of Hebrews 4:14-15:

> Therefore, since we have a great high priest who has ascended into heaven, Jesus the Son of God, let us hold firmly to the faith we profess. For we do not have a high priest who is unable to empathize with our weaknesses, but we have one who has been tempted in every way, just as we are—yet he did not sin.

Then explore other New Testament passages that also support the idea of Jesus' sinlessness, such as the following:

> He "had no sin." (2 Corinthians 5:11-21)
> He "committed no sin." (1 Peter 2:21-25)
> In him "is no sin." (1 John 3:4-6)

Once you've done this, teach the Gospel stories that cause young people to call into question the belief that Jesus was sinless. Since teens connect Jesus' anti-establishment behavior with sin, wrestle with Jesus' words in Matthew 22:20-22: "So give back to Caesar what is Caesar's, and to God what is God's." In light of those words, ask teens: *Can we really call Jesus anti-establishment? If we can, then is being anti-establishment necessarily sinful behavior?*

Similarly, since teens cite Jesus' willingness to heal people on the Sabbath as an example of sin, wrestle with Matthew

5:17 and how Jesus did not come to "abolish the laws or the prophets" but to fulfill them. Again, ask teens: *If Jesus came to fulfill the law, then was it really sinful for him to heal on the Sabbath? How might such an act have actually fulfilled the law?*

In the same way, since research participants distinguished between Jesus' actions and his thoughts, explore Jesus' words in the Sermon on the Mount. Look at how in this passage Jesus broadens the traditional interpretation of the Ten Commandments to include sinful thoughts. Then debate whether or not it's really possible for us to differentiate between sinful thoughts and actions.

Likewise, wrestle in depth with the story of Jesus cleansing the temple in Matthew 21:12-16. Do so together in community, in a space where it's safe for young people to ask and answer questions about this story.

Give teens the context of this passage. Explain how merchants were selling items people needed in order to offer their sacrifices and fulfill the Old Testament laws. Challenge teens to imagine what this scene would have been like. Don't gloss over or attempt to justify Jesus' rage. Instead, dwell on it. Ask teens: *What must Jesus have been feeling to push over the tables of the money changers?* and *How do you think the temple merchants reacted to Jesus' rage?* Wrestle with whether or not emotions like anger are really sins. Use other Scripture passages to further this conversation. Consider, for example, Ephesians 4:25-27, which says: "In your anger do not sin: Do not let the sun go down while you are still angry, and do not give the devil a foothold."

Since teens are sometimes more familiar with the Ten Commandments than they are with the Jesus story, build upon that familiarity. When I look at the story of Jesus

70

cleansing the temple, I don't see him breaking any of the Ten Commandments. I do, however, see him upholding several of them. So go through the Ten Commandments one by one and ask teens to identify which commandment Jesus broke when he overturned the tables in the temple. Then challenge them to consider which of the commandments Jesus' actions actually upheld. Once you've done that, debate whether Jesus' actions in this story are an act of defiance or obedience.

To further help teens understand Jesus' motivations in this story, instead of skimming over the rest of it, include the quote Jesus gives in Matthew 21:13 about it being a "house of prayer," and really dig into it. Return to the quote's original source in Isaiah 56:7— "Their burnt offerings and their sacrifices will be accepted on my altar for my house shall be called a house of prayer for all nations." Wrestle with what this passage would have meant to people in Isaiah's time and to Jews in Jesus' time who would have been familiar with the words of this prophet.

Then get personal. Challenge teens to imagine how Jesus would react if he entered your worship space on a given Sunday. Consider the various things you "sell"—coffee, baked goods, or even books. Even though such sales no doubt benefit worthy causes, ask teens if they think Jesus would react to this in the same way he did to the merchants in the temple. If teens say yes, challenge them to wrestle with how they—and your church—can respond to this. If teens say no, ask them how the merchandising in your church is different from that found in the ancient temple. Finally, challenge teens to think about the purpose of the temple—of their church—and how we do and don't make it a "house of prayer" today.

EMBRACE DOUBT

Throughout your conversations with teens, make space for their doubts. For young people to take ownership of their faith, they must be able to question it and wrestle through those issues that are central to it, yet are often tough to understand. Rather than fear doubt, embrace it, just as Jesus seemed to do with Thomas in John 20:24-29.

Together with your teens in your ministry, wrestle with this story and in particular with Jesus' words to Thomas, "Do not doubt but believe." So often, we interpret those words to mean it's wrong for us to doubt. But is that really what they mean?

Discuss how Jesus meets Thomas in the middle of his doubts and how Jesus might meet them in the middle of their doubts and questions. Wrestle with the questions teens have about their faith. After all, as author Madeleine L'Engle said, "If religion is true, it will stand up to all my questioning; there is no need to fear."[9]

Show young people it's okay to doubt and give them permission to ask questions and express doubt. As part of this, share your own doubts (past or present) to help show teens they are not alone in their doubt. Help them understand, as Andrew Root does, that doubt "may not be a tumor but the very organ of faith surrounded by the tissue of fear, brokenness, and suffering."[10]

EXPLORE CHEAP GRACE

Since teens argued Jesus sinned because "he knew all along that your sins would be forgiven," wrestle with whether or not we ever do the same by discussing cheap grace. Explore Paul's words in Romans 6:1—"What shall we say, then? Shall we go on sinning so that grace may increase?" As part of this conversation, wrestle with why we sin in the first place; why we continue to sin; and how we can and should respond to grace. As you do, define grace—through both your words and actions. When teens mess up (which they will!), show them grace. (We'll talk more about this in in chapter 6.) Give them second, third, and fiftieth chances even (and especially) when they don't deserve it.

As you show teens grace, help them process their emotions. Work through residual guilt with them, helping them understand grace is never about what they deserve. Just as Jesus challenges the adulterous woman in John 8 to "go and sin no more" after he showed her grace, challenge teens to go and do likewise. Not because they must, but because that's the natural response to extravagant grace. As our youth begin to understand the type of life grace naturally prompts, the notion that one might sin because we know we'll be forgiven will seem increasingly ludicrous.

PAINT AN ACCURATE PICTURE OF JESUS' RELATIONSHIP WITH GOD

One of the many things that surprised me during my conversations with young people was how frequently those who believed that Jesus sinned then tried to justify his sin. According to one of them, "You don't talk to God if you don't sin."

How does this young person know this?

Maybe it's because *he* doesn't talk to God when he's not sinning.

Perhaps this adolescent's prayer life looks a little something like this: "Hey, God. Remember me? Well, I screwed up again. I yelled at my mom and cheated on my math test. Please forgive me." In all likelihood, this young man's prayer life doesn't include prayers of thanksgiving or even prayers for others. Instead, it's probably consumed with confession and forgiveness. Since this is what his prayer life consists of, he's naturally concluded, "You don't talk to God if you don't sin." Rather than seeing himself as being made in the image of God, he's essentially created Jesus in *his* image.

To remedy this, talk about the relationship between Jesus and God shown in Scripture. Investigate Jesus' baptism, those times when he retreats to be alone with his Father, and his agonizingly beautiful prayer in the garden of Gethsemane. Highlight Jesus' dependence on God as well as their interconnectedness. Emphasize why Jesus talked to God.

As you study these passages, create a list of the different reasons why Jesus talked to God. Then model these different things as you pray with teens in your ministry. (We'll talk more about this in chapter 11.) Doing so will help them see prayer is about more than just confession. Doing so will debunk the myth that "you don't talk to God if you don't sin." It will also paint a more realistic picture of the kind of relationship Jesus had with God, as well as the kind of relationship we can have with him.

Additionally, use this to launch a discussion about what a healthy relationship with Jesus entails. Help teens understand that healthy relationships aren't one-sided. In a healthy relationship, you don't stop talking to someone; you don't spend time with someone only when you need something. As you discuss healthy relationships, remember that many teens have not experienced this kind of relationship with anyone yet, including Jesus. As a result, unashamedly use examples of real-life relationships to illustrate what healthy relationships look like, both with Jesus and others.

HIS PERFECTION, NOT OURS

Ultimately, my hope for the church and, in particular, for those in our youth ministries is that strengthening this aspect of our Christologies will give us the freedom and courage to stop trying to be perfect and instead recognize and worship Jesus, the one who was and is perfect.

CHAPTER NOTES

1. Brennan Manning, *The Ragamuffin Gospel* (Sisters, OR: Multnomah Publishers, 2000), 132.

2. David Kinnaman, *You Lost Me: Why Young Christians Are Leaving Church and Rethinking Faith* (Grand Rapids, MI: Baker Books, 2011), 24.

3. Thom S. Rainer and Jess W. Rainer, *The Millennials: Connecting to America's Largest Generation* (Nashville: B&H Publishing Group, 2011), 242.

4. Mike Nappa, *The Jesus Survey: What Christian Teens Really Believe and Why* (Grand Rapids, MI: Baker Books, 2012), 31.

5. Scot McKnight, *The Blue Parakeet: Rethinking How You Read the Bible* (Grand Rapids, MI: Zondervan, 2008), 66.

6. Joseph M. Scriven, "What a Friend We Have in Jesus" (Song Lyrics), 1855.

7. Rick Lawrence, *Jesus-Centered Youth Ministry: Moving from Jesus-Plus to Jesus-Only* (Loveland, CO: Group Publishing, 2014), 136.

8. Ibid., 147.

9. Madeleine L'Engle, *Walking on Water: Reflections on Faith and Art* (Wheaton, IL: Harold Shaw Publishers, 1980), 156.

10. Andrew Root and Kenda Creasy Dean, *The Theological Turn in Youth Ministry* (Downers Grove, IL: InterVarsity Press, 2011).

CHAPTER 4

JESUS: THE GOOD NEWS

A few days after I completed eighth grade, my uncle was diagnosed with terminal lung cancer. The doctors said there was no hope; but as a young Christian, I knew they were wrong. I knew that with God, all things were possible. So I prayed for a miracle and continued praying for a miracle right up until the day he died, six months later.

While my uncle was still battling cancer, my paternal grandma was diagnosed with it as well. Once again, the doctors said there was no hope. Their hopelessness drove me to my knees, where I prayed fervently for a miracle. A few months later, she too died.

Ten years later, my grandpa was diagnosed with cancer. Again, the doctors said he was terminal. This time around I still prayed, but with a little less fervor than before—a bit unsure as to whether or not God was still in the business of doing miracles. A few months later, Grandpa died.

Two years after that, my maternal grandma was diagnosed with Lou Gehrig's disease, one of the nastiest diseases imaginable. With no cure and very few treatment options available, Lou Gehrig's disease is a death sentence. Despite that, once again, I begged God to do something. A few months later, she died as well.

No doubt, some of you will argue that in each of those instances God did, in fact, perform a miracle. He brought my family together, gave us moments of joy amidst seasons of sorrow, and even gave us small victories along the way. Yet, in each of these instances, God failed to do the one thing I asked him to do. Four times I asked God to heal someone I loved, and not once did he oblige. By the fourth time, I'd begun to wonder, *Did I do something wrong? Did I not have enough faith? Or has God left the miracle business altogether?*

I've had enough conversations with people to know I'm not alone in this. How often have you prayed—in faith—for the impossible to happen? How often have you begged God to show up and make himself known in the face of tragedy?

Maybe, like me, during times of tragedy you fall to your knees and pray for a miracle. Perhaps the teens in your youth ministry do the same. I know many in mine do. Yet, the truth is, few of us have ever seen a miracle—at least not in the form of a complete healing, against all odds.

WHAT TEENS BELIEVE ABOUT JESUS' MIRACLES

Despite how infrequently we bear witness to miracles in our own lives, when push comes to shove, most of us still *want* to believe miracles happen. We long for the impossible to become reality. Maybe that's why when I asked high school students if Jesus performed miracles, 95 percent of them said he did. When I specifically asked them if Jesus rose from the dead, an overwhelming 96 percent of those I surveyed said he did. Other research also supports young people's overwhelming belief in the resurrection. According to researcher Mike Nappa, 83 percent of teens "strongly affirm that Jesus rose from the dead."[1]

Intrigued by how large a percentage of adolescents said Jesus rose from the dead, I wanted to see if there were any subsets within my larger population who all said this was true. To find out, I treated each congregation I visited as an individual group and analyzed their responses to this question, something I then did for every other question on the survey as well. Doing so revealed this was the only question on the survey for which repeated subsets expressed any degree of certainty in their answers. In three out of the four congregations that participated in my research, all the young people surveyed said Jesus rose from the dead. (See Figure 5.) This was true of the Bible Belt, small town, and rural congregations I visited.

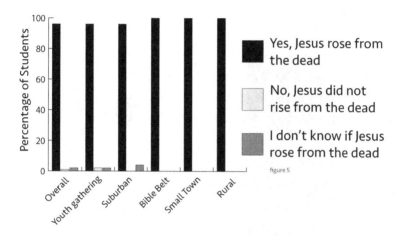

figure 5

To be honest, when I first saw these numbers, I let out a deep sigh of relief. After so much disheartening news, this felt to me as though I was finally discovering some good news in regard to teens' Christologies. These young people may not know Jesus is God. They may not know Jesus was perfect. But at least they know Jesus rose from the dead.

Read those last three sentences again, though, and perhaps you'll start to see what I did: This may not be such good news after all. That such a high percentage of young people agreed Jesus rose from the dead means many did so even though they don't think Jesus is God.

Having realized this, I began comparing adolescents' answers to the question of whether or not Jesus rose from the dead with their answers to the question: *Is Jesus God?* (See Figure 6.) When I did, I found that nearly half of those surveyed (43 percent) affirmed that Jesus was God and that he rose from the dead. The problem is, an equal percentage (43 percent) believed in the resurrection even though they didn't believe Jesus was God.

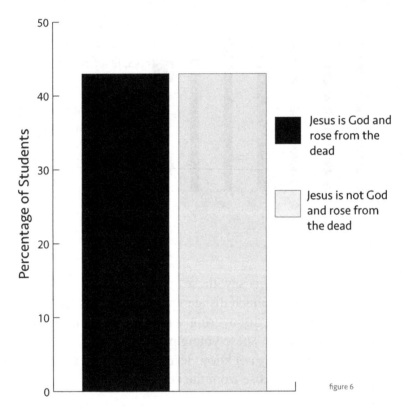

figure 6

Baffled by how people could believe Jesus rose from the dead if he wasn't God, I asked young people: *If Jesus isn't God, then how can he save us?* One of the teens who shared her logic said: "God was in Jesus. He was like a puppet for God that was supposed to come down to earth and show everyone what he could do." This same girl went on to elaborate that as a puppet ultimately controlled by God, it was possible for Jesus to have accomplished God's mission—including his death and

80

resurrection—even though he, himself, was not actually God. In many ways, such reasoning reflects a belief in the Superhero Jesus we explored in chapter 1. Though Superhero Jesus isn't God, his superhero powers allow him to perform superhuman feats, like raising himself from the dead.

A CRASH COURSE IN ATONEMENT THEORIES

In Christianity, we use the word *atonement* to describe the doctrine concerning the reconciliation of God and humankind, especially as accomplished through the life, suffering, and death of Jesus. Several different atonement theories are commonly used to explain why Jesus died.

Arguably, the two most common atonement theories in American churches are the substitutionary atonement theory and the ransom theory. The substitutionary atonement theory argues that Jesus was punished in the place of sinners, thereby satisfying the demands of justice from a holy God. The ransom theory says Jesus was a ransom paid to Satan in exchange for the souls held captive as a result of sin.

Both the substitutionary and ransom atonement theories are rooted in Scripture. One of the key passages used to support the substitutionary view of atonement is Romans 3:23-26.

> For all have sinned and fall short of the glory of God, and all are justified freely by his grace through the redemption that came by Christ Jesus. God presented Christ as a sacrifice of atonement, through the shedding of his blood—to be received by faith. He did this to demonstrate his righteousness, because in his forbearance he had left the sins committed beforehand unpunished—he did it to demonstrate his righteousness at the present time, so as to be just and the one who justifies those who have faith in Jesus.

In comparison, 1 Timothy 2:5-6a is commonly used to support the ransom theory of atonement: "For there is one God and one mediator between God and mankind, the man Christ Jesus, who gave himself as a ransom for all people."

WHY DID JESUS DIE?

Since the atonement and our understanding of Jesus' death and resurrection is central to Christianity, I thought it was important to do more than just ask participants to respond to the multiple-choice question: *Did Jesus rise from the dead?* So I also asked them to answer the short-answer question of why Jesus died. Their answers are depicted visually in the word cloud below. (See Figure 7.) There, the responses young people gave most frequently are largest and boldest.

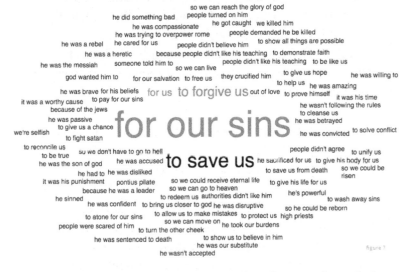

figure 7

Despite having the freedom to respond to the question of why Jesus died, using whatever language they wanted, the majority (70 percent) said some variation of the idea that Jesus died "for our sins."

The next most frequently given responses were …

- Jesus died "to save us."
- Jesus died "to forgive us."
- Jesus died so we can have eternal life or "go to heaven."
- Jesus died "for us."
- Jesus died "to free us."

And the very pragmatic …

- Jesus died because "they crucified him."

Not surprisingly, teens' most prevalent responses to the question of why Jesus died corresponded to the most dominant atonement theories of our time. The prevalence of the substitutionary atonement theory is reflected in the fact that the majority of those I surveyed said Jesus died "for our sins." Similarly, those who spoke of Jesus dying in order to "free us" described the ransom theory of atonement.

It's worth noting that since nearly three-quarters of the high school students I surveyed believed Jesus died for their sins, many did so even though they didn't believe Jesus was sinless. In fact, three-quarters of those who said Jesus was an imperfect God still said Jesus died "for our sins." Similarly, two-thirds of those who concluded Jesus was an imperfect human agreed he died "for our sins."

Once again, to better understand this seemingly contradictory response, I asked the youth in my focus groups: *What role does Jesus play in the forgiveness of sins?* According to one:

When Jesus died, all of our sins were forgiven. We still need to ask for that forgiveness. You're not going to be given it automatically. But when you ask, God is gracious and will forgive you of your sins. That was Jesus' ultimate purpose in our lives.

Even when pushed about how an imperfect being could forgive sins, young people held firm in their beliefs, confident that "by the grace of God, all of our wrong doing is forgiven."

MATH THAT DOESN'T MAKE SENSE

To teens, atonement theories are too often the equivalent of saying $2 + 2 = 6$. They are math equations that don't add up.

Consider this: One young person I interviewed, then a senior, explained how throughout her life she'd been told Jesus died for her sins. To this girl, that made no sense. In her words, "I don't get it."

She went on to explain that she didn't understand how the death of someone—even someone who was sinless—could make up for her sins. Among other things, this girl, a deep thinker, was frustrated by how simplistic the church had made Jesus' death. According to her, "I just think there's gotta be more to this."

REINTRODUCE MYSTERY

Therein lies the problem with many atonement theories. They are, at their core, reductionist. They're designed to make complex ideas easily understandable.

Don't get me wrong. From a developmental standpoint, this is critically important for teens. Yet, at the same time, teens are drawn to the mysterious, which many mainline denominations recognize during worship by saying, "Let us proclaim the mystery of faith: Christ has died, Christ is risen, Christ will come again." It's no wonder teens struggle with atonement theories that, at their core, rob faith of its mystery.

Perhaps one way to put the mystery back into faith is to teach multiple atonement theories. Now, before you accuse me of heresy, let me explain. For centuries, the church has adhered to a variety of different atonement theories besides the two dominant ones found in churches today. Those that have survived the test of time are all rooted in Scripture.

Given this, perhaps we'd do well to acknowledge the complexity and the mystery of Jesus' death and resurrection; to talk about how it's possible to believe something that is, at its core, difficult, if not impossible, to explain.

What would happen if we explained Jesus' death and resurrection using the substitutionary atonement theory one week, and the ransom theory of atonement the next? What if we also discussed lesser-known atonement theories, like the representative model of atonement?

According to this view of atonement, Jesus does not replace us. Carl Braaten says:

> Christ suffered for us, but he did not suffer instead of us. We still have to suffer. Christ died for us, but he did not die instead of us; we still have to die. He is not our substitute in the sense that he replaces us. He is qualified by his life, death, and resurrection to be our representative. He has the right credentials to be the ambassador of the human race before God.[2]

Jesus is, Braaten reasons, not only the representative of humankind before God, but also God's representative before humankind. After all, he says:

> God needs to have a representative to plead his case in an unbelieving age that asks, "If God exists and if God is in charge, why does he allow innocent people

to suffer and die? Why does he allow bad things to happen to good people?"[3]

To put it another way, think of Jesus in this view of atonement as an interpreter. For example, for five years I worked at a multi-ethnic church. I'm Caucasian, but nearly all of my youth were Korean. Many of their parents were born in Korea; others were the first generation to be born in the United States. Throughout my ministry in this congregation, I often found myself baffled by differences in our cultural customs. Such differences sometimes inhibited my ministry.

Thankfully, one of the adult leaders in my ministry acted as an interpreter between the Korean parents and me. This leader was born in Korea but raised in the United States. Her birthplace, as well as the cultural customs she grew up with, gave her the appropriate credentials to relate to and connect with Korean parents in a way I simply could not. At the same time, because she was raised in the United States, she understood me and my cultural customs in a way the parents could not. As a result, she could represent me to the Korean parents while also representing them to me.

Such is the role Jesus plays in the representative view of atonement.

Of course, there's no guarantee teens will grasp an alternative version of the atonement any more than they will the substitutionary or ransom theories of atonement. But it seems to me that in the same way we increase our ability to relate to different types of students when we teach with multiple learning styles in mind, we'll also increase our ability to help teens understand the atonement when we explain Jesus' death and resurrection using multiple analogies and illustrations.

Consider, for a moment, the girl for whom the substitutionary theory of atonement represented math that didn't equate. For 18 years this girl had listened to people tell her that Jesus' death paid for her sins. Yet it still didn't make sense to her. Maybe, however, a different atonement theory would have. Maybe this girl would have resonated with the language of the ransom theory of atonement or maybe the representative model of atonement would have made complete sense to her and, as a result, drawn her closer to Jesus—giving her a new way to make sense of and explain his death and resurrection.

TAKE OFF JESUS' SUPERHERO CAPE

As you reintroduce mystery into your teaching about Jesus' death and resurrection, simultaneously ground teens in your youth ministry in reality. To do this, help them develop a more complete picture of Jesus than the archetypes presented in chapter 1.

Though at first glance the Superhero Jesus archetype might not seem all that different from the Orthodox Jesus described in Scripture, in truth, it's far from complete. By nature, superheroes derive their power from something else. Spider-man's power comes from the venom of an irradiated spider; Superman's comes from a yellow star. Thus, it's only natural for teens to conclude that Superhero Jesus derives his power from elsewhere; that when he performs miracles, he does so because he's received that power *from* God, not because he *is* God.

So in order to correct that misconception and help teens connect Jesus' miracles—including his resurrection—to his divinity, take off his superhero cape. Whenever you explore one of Jesus' miracles, intentionally discuss the source of his power. Help teens understand that while, ultimately, all power comes from God, Jesus' power was not external but internal. Because he *is* God. As part of this, explore how Jesus' miracles authenticate his divinity.

DRAW SOME SHEEP

Clearly, I think it's important to reintroduce mystery into our teaching about Jesus' death and resurrection. That said, I also think it's vitally important to recognize where young people are at developmentally.

As we discussed in chapter 2, high school teens have only just begun to think abstractly. And what's more abstract than the atonement?

This means when we talk about Jesus' death and resurrection with young people, we have to make this abstract concept concrete. This starts with avoiding incomprehensible words like *atonement*.

It also means we can't say things like: "Jesus was punished in place of sinners, thereby satisfying the demands of justice from a holy God." If you say that, I guarantee teens won't understand what you're talking about. Just think how confused the girl I interviewed was, and that was after she'd heard this explanation throughout her life.

So break down this theory. Start by talking about the Old Testament laws regarding sacrifices. Draw some sheep and explain how many sheep people had to sacrifice in order to make amends for their sins. Elaborate on the condition those sheep had to be in for those sacrifices to be acceptable.

Then talk about the first Passover. Discuss why the Israelites were required to sacrifice an unblemished lamb (and talk about what the word *unblemished* means in the first place). Finally, turn to the New Testament. Explore passages that refer to Jesus' sinlessness, like the ones we discussed in chapter 3. Talk about how he, like the first Passover lamb, was unblemished. Then talk about the new covenant and how Jesus' death and the shedding of his blood fulfilled the Old Testament sacrificial laws.

MAKE IT RELATIONAL

Regardless of which atonement theories you teach, be careful not to reduce Jesus' death and resurrection to a formula. After all, our Christian faith is, at its heart, relational. So, too, is Jesus' death and resurrection. In fact, in John 15:13, Jesus describes his imminent death in relational terms, saying, "Greater love has no one than this: to lay down one's life for one's friends."

As you help teens wrestle with the meaning behind Jesus' death and resurrection, don't lose sight of the fact that his death was an act of great love for us. Even though 10 percent of the teens I surveyed believe Jesus died so we can go to heaven, Jesus' death and resurrection is, in actuality, about far more than our entrance to heaven; it's about more than just a Get Out of Hell Free Card, regardless of how often we try to make it exactly that.

Consider the Sinner's Prayer. I prayed that prayer as a sophomore in college. I did so despite having grown up in the church and despite having believed in Jesus for as long as I could remember. That year, however, the Christian crowd I was hanging out with informed me there was a prayer you had to pray in order to become a Christian. In it, you confessed your sins, stated your need for a Savior, and acknowledged that Jesus was that Savior who died on the cross and rose from the dead to save you from your sins. Once prayed, your fate was sealed and you were bound for heaven.

Imagine my friends' surprise when they discovered that, despite being raised in a church and calling myself a Christian, I'd never prayed this prayer. They were horrified and feared my soul was in grave danger.

Since I figured it couldn't hurt to say a bunch of things I already believed, I said the Sinner's Prayer.

My friends rejoiced, convinced they'd saved me from the fires of hell.

I suppose there's a chance they did.

Even so, when I look back on that day, I feel as though that prayer actually cheapened my relationship with Jesus by making it about one thing, and one thing only: my entrance to heaven.

Now, don't get me wrong. I think we should celebrate teens when they confess their belief in Jesus, whether it's for the first or the hundredth time. I think we should rejoice when they make or reaffirm their commitments to follow Jesus in their daily lives. But I also think we have to help our youth understand that such a commitment isn't just about heaven; it's about now. To do that, we've got to help them understand that Jesus' death and resurrection matters beyond our salvation.

TEACH THE THEOLOGY OF THE CROSS

One of the best ways to help teens understand that Jesus' death and resurrection matters beyond our salvation is to teach them the theology of the cross. Pulling from Braaten again, according to this theology, had God been unwilling to be "edged out of the world and onto the cross," he would have been of no use and help to humankind.[4] Instead, it's only by becoming "weak and powerless in the world" that God can be with us and help us.[5]

Through the cross, God is with us. Because of the cross, God can help us—not just in the future, but now. If that's true, then Jesus' death and resurrection should impact every aspect of our daily lives.

Consider this story. Recently, I led a retreat on sexuality for a group of high school teens. During this retreat, I asked the group to rank a list of sexual activities, deciding for themselves *when* in a relationship each sexual act was acceptable and how far was too far outside of marriage. After seeing their responses, I asked the teens: *How does your relationship with Jesus influence the decision you're making regarding sex?*

My hope is that my question caused the youth to think about what impact Jesus' death and resurrection has on their sexual ethics.

Because it should have one.

Jesus' death and resurrection is one of the foundations of our faith. Therefore, what we believe about it shapes crucial aspects of our identity, our faith, and even our actions—not just in the afterlife, but in the present one as well.

CHAPTER NOTES

1. Mike Nappa, *The Jesus Survey: What Christian Teens Really Believe and Why* (Grand Rapids, MI: Baker Books, 2012), 61.
2. Carl E. Braaten, *Who Is Jesus? Disputed Questions and Answers* (Grand Rapids, MI: William B. Eerdmans Publishing Company, 2011), 106.
3. Ibid.
4. Ibid., 96.
5. Ibid.

CHAPTER 5
JESUS: AN OPTIONAL PART OF CHRISTIANITY

For quite some time, *tolerance* has been a popular buzzword in the United States. Everyone—especially high school students—wants to be tolerant of one another.

Organizations like businesses and universities now even teach tolerance, believing that doing so will promote diversity and end problems like bullying. Such thinking is also pervasive in elementary schools, junior highs, and high schools around the United States.

A few years ago, one of the local high schools in my community sponsored a "Mix It Up at Lunch Day" program to teach tolerance.[1] This program, created by the Southern Poverty Law Center, encouraged students to "mix it up" by taking a new seat in the cafeteria at lunch. The hope was to challenge students to cross the lines of division in their schools, meet new people, and (ultimately) build an inclusive and welcoming community.

Not long after this event, my high school students and I were wrestling with whether or not all religions were the same. During this discussion, I noticed some of them becoming more and more uncomfortable. Eventually, I asked what was going on. One then shared how merely taking part in our conversation made her feel as though she were being intolerant of others. Several others echoed her sentiment, saying other people automatically assume they, as Christians, are intolerant.

And to this generation, there's no label worse than "intolerant."

WHAT TEENS BELIEVE ABOUT JESUS' ROLE IN CHRISTIANITY

Given how much teens fear being labeled "intolerant," it's not surprising that on the surveys, when I asked if it were possible to be a Christian and not believe in Jesus, nearly one-third responded yes. To them, it's possible to be a Christian without believing in the one on whom Christianity is based. An additional quarter of those surveyed responded "I don't know" to this question, leaving only 42 percent who affirmed that Jesus is crucial to the Christian faith. (See Figure 8.)

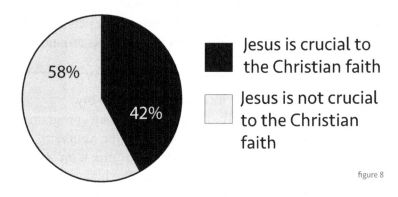

58%

42%

Jesus is crucial to the Christian faith

Jesus is not crucial to the Christian faith

figure 8

Other research also supports these findings. One out of three young people surveyed by Mike Nappa affirm that Jesus, Mohammad, Buddha, and other great religious leaders all have equal standing in leading people to heaven.[2] The book *Millennials: Connecting to America's Largest Generation* by Thom Rainer and Jess Rainer analyzes and reports on LifeWay's Millennial Study, in which only 31 percent of Millennials agree Jesus is the only way to heaven.[3] Similarly, in *You Lost Me*, researcher David Kinnaman concludes 18-to-29-year-olds are "more likely than the previous generation of Americans to believe in religious pluralism, which holds there are many different paths to God."[4]

Other research suggests this phenomenon is not unique to Millennials. According to one study described in the book *American Grace: How Religion Divides and Unites Us*: "Most Americans who belong to Christian faiths told us they believe non-Christians can go to heaven. Of those who said people of other faiths could attain salvation, 89 percent of Catholics, [and] 82 percent of mainline Protestants ... say that salvation extends to non-Christians."[5]

In yet another survey—this one conducted by authors Greg Hawkins and Cally Parkinson for their book *Move: What 1,000 Churches Reveal About Spiritual Growth*—one respondent admitted: "It's not that I don't believe in Jesus, but I struggle with believing there's only one path to God. I wonder about things like, if God is all-forgiving, then why won't you go to heaven if you don't believe in Christ?"[6]

WHAT DOES IT MEAN TO BE A CHRISTIAN?

As I dug deeper into my own data, I noticed the percentage of those who said it was possible to be a Christian without believing in Jesus or who didn't know how crucial Jesus was to the Christian faith (58 percent) is very similar to the percentage who either believed Jesus was not God, or didn't know if Jesus was God (56 percent)—something we discussed in chapter 2. Since these percentages were so similar, I compared young people's answers to these two questions with one another. Doing so revealed 12 percent of high school students believed Jesus isn't necessary to the Christian faith even though they believed he's God. For those individuals, what does it mean to be a Christian?

To find out, I asked young people during my focus groups what they thought it meant to be a Christian. Most of those I spoke with defined Christianity as faith in God, not necessarily in Jesus. According to one, "What sets us apart is our God. Some people might have a different God or have a different story of God. Knowing where your God came from and knowing what he did for you makes you a Christian." Likewise, another young person had the vague sense that being a Christian meant knowing there's "someone out there who created us." Another suggested, "Christians believe that God will be with you anytime, anywhere, and help you through."

For some of those in my focus groups, Jesus was actually completely irrelevant to the Christian faith. One suburban teen put it like this, "I believe you can be a Christian without knowing about Jesus, just by knowing there's something after all this."

Another factor often used to define Christianity is culture. An interview with one Millennial, Brandon, during LifeWay's Millennial Study illustrates this.

> When we asked Brandon if he was a Christian, he responded quickly, "Sure I am." We knew better than to accept that response at face value, so we asked him to articulate his Christian beliefs. "Well, most Americans are Christians, and so I guess I am too," he began. "I think my parents are Christians, but I've never really asked them. I have a pretty good feel for Jesus. I'm sure he was a good man like most religious leaders."[7]

A cultural definition of Christianity is certainly not limited to Millennials. In Hawkins and Parkinson's study of 250,000 congregants attending 1,000 churches for *Move*, they discovered that even though many parishioners report that Jesus is "not important" in their lives, many would say (and do believe, according to the researchers) that they are Christians. This suggests, the authors assert, that many people fail to grasp the basic premise of the Christian faith, despite the fact that churches often intentionally define Christianity as "the practice of believing in and following Jesus."[8]

Such beliefs seem to be growing in prevalence even though churches still claim to adhere to an orthodox understanding that Jesus is the only way to salvation. In a recent study of the Evangelical Free Church of America, youth ministry professor and researcher Len Kageler asked youth workers to choose one of three answers (*yes, not sure,* or *not really*) in response to this statement: "I believe Jesus Christ is the only way of salvation, that only Christianity, no other religions or religious leaders, provide a way for salvation and heaven." All 70 youth pastors chose yes, and 91 percent of them indicated they teach this more than once a year.[9]

Unfortunately, that message is getting through to only a small number of churched teenagers. At my focus groups when teens were asked what it meant to be a Christian, those who mentioned "belief in Jesus" were in the minority. According to one, "Being a Christian [means] you accept that Jesus died for our sins. He saved us." Another said being a Christian means "following Jesus and knowing he has a plan for you." Yet another teen elaborated, saying, "You do what Jesus does. Not necessarily that if you go to church, you're a Christian. I don't personally think it works that way."

WHAT MUST SOMEONE BELIEVE ABOUT JESUS TO BE A CHRISTIAN?

Since most of those who attended my focus groups didn't specifically use Jesus to define Christianity, I also explicitly asked: *What must someone believe about Jesus to be a Christian?*

Many young people set this bar very low. According to one, you must believe Jesus was real: "He existed and what he did happened." Another added, "Believe that what he did was for you, not just certain people."

In some instances, youth avoided answering this question by defaulting to doctrine. One explained, "One of the main things you should do is the Ten Commandments, the Lord's Prayer, and the Apostles' Creed. You should follow them as best as you can." After a great deal of lively conversation about this, another concluded, "It just depends on what you believe. It's different for every person in [his or her] view of faith."

JESUS IS OPTIONAL

The fact that our culture highly values tolerance is seen in that particular teen's statement: "It just depends on what you believe. It's different for every person in [his or her] view of faith." Like so many of her peers, this teen believes faith is different for everyone; that even for Christians, Jesus is optional.

Once again, this fits with researcher Mike Nappa's conclusion: "The overarching value of supposed tolerance for other religions has somewhat trumped the value of truth, making it natural for our Christian students to actually deny their own beliefs when they may be perceived (rightly or wrongly) as intolerant."[10]

THE IMPACT OF GLOBALIZATION

At the same time our society is increasingly valuing tolerance, high school teens are becoming more globalized. Many high schools are more diverse than they've ever been. As a result, teens are not only interacting with those whose religious beliefs differ from their own, but they're also forming deep relationships with them. Additionally, many high school curriculums include a unit on world religions. During this unit, Christianity is presented as one of many equally acceptable religious options alongside Islam, Hinduism, and Buddhism. Even young adults surrounded by individuals who are just like them have—through the advent of the Internet and, in particular, social-networking sites—unprecedented opportunities to follow, learn from, and be in relationship with people from other cultures and religions. Likewise, frequent and relatively affordable flights make it possible for teens to go anywhere they want in a short amount of time. This, in turn, has given teens access to places and people that even a generation ago, would have been considered largely off-limits. Such opportunities are not merely limited to vacations, but have become increasingly important for work, school (study abroad), and—thanks to the advent of short-term mission trips—ministry.

When combined with our society's value of tolerance, this increased globalization often causes teens to unite around (and even celebrate) the similarities they share with those of other nationalities, cultures, and religions. By focusing on their similarities, teens are able to easily accept others. Unfortunately, they also tend to lose sight of what or who distinguishes and differentiates their religion from every other religion that exists in the world: Jesus.

RAISE THE BAR

Helping teens differentiate their Christian faith from all other world religions begins with taking the steps we've already discussed in chapters 2 through 4 to strengthen their basic Christologies (something we'll talk even more about in section 2). Without becoming overly legalistic, let's raise the bar on what we expect teens to know about Jesus. Let's make it our goal for the teens who graduate from our ministries to leave knowing more than just "Jesus was real."

Why?

Because what we know and believe about someone or something affects how we live.

STOP TEACHING TOLERANCE

Beyond that, to help teens understand that Jesus is a central rather than optional part of their Christian faith, differentiate between love and tolerance. Help teens understand tolerance is a cultural value, not a biblical one. God never says, "Tolerate your neighbor." Jesus does, however, command: "Love your neighbor." What's more, he takes that one step further and says, "Love your enemies and pray for those who persecute you" (Matthew 5:44).

Remind teens that sometimes love will do what tolerance cannot. While tolerance might get someone to "mix it up" at lunch and sit with different people for a mere 30 minutes one day, it doesn't teach young people to actually respect those who are different from them. In reality, it doesn't even teach them to like those who are different than them. It's entirely possible to tolerate someone you despise.

Tolerance also doesn't teach young people to embrace differences and learn from them. It doesn't teach them to find the inherent dignity and worth of a person that comes from being created in God's image, regardless of ethnicity or socioeconomic status. Tolerance aims to unite people over how they are the same, but love reaches out and embraces what makes us different. Tolerance doesn't teach forgiveness or true acceptance, but love does.

After helping teens distinguish between tolerance and love, investigate together what else Scripture says about love. Read John 13:34-35, where Jesus calls love the defining characteristic of Christians:

> A new command I give you: Love one another. As I have loved you, so you must love one another. By this everyone will know that you are my disciples, if you

love one another.

Since love is the defining mark of a Christian, help teens wrestle with how love manifests itself in their lives, and in particular, with how to show love to those who are different from them. Point out when you see teens loving others versus when you see them tolerating others. Ask them to self-reflect on this idea as well.

TEACH "WE" NOT "I"

As I traveled around the country hosting focus groups, I was struck by how frequently the participants I talked to used singular rather than plural pronouns to describe their beliefs, especially as we discussed what role, if any, Jesus plays in distinguishing the Christian faith from others.

So often, youth began their responses with: "Other people might disagree, *but I believe ...*" Or: "*What I believe is ...*" In contrast, no one ever responded to my questions about an issue by saying, *"We believe ..."*

As a youth worker, this excited me. As I'm sure you do, I want my teens to be able to articulate their personal beliefs; to make statements about what they as individuals believe about Jesus, and to own those beliefs—regardless of whether or not their friends or families share them.

Yet, as a researcher, I fear this is not what was actually happening. To me, this felt like something different—like a way for teens to assert their personal beliefs in a world in which they fear doing so will cause others to view them as intolerant. By defaulting to first-person language, teens are making it clear that this is what *they* believe, not necessarily what they think *you* ought to believe. After all, they know that what works for them may not necessarily work for you.

One way to counter this is to emphasize the communal over the individual. Learn from the words of the Nicene Creed, which boldly declare, "*We* believe in one Lord, Jesus Christ, the only Son of God ..." In particular, do this when discussing doctrine. Instead of sharing only what *you* believe, also share what *your church* believes. This is especially important when discussing controversial issues. While it's okay to give your opinion on an issue, be equally quick to share, "Here's our church's belief on this issue." In the same way, whenever teens respond to your faith questions with "I" statements, ask them how their personal beliefs compare with others'. Challenge them to know and express not only their individual, but also their communal faith in Jesus.

In addition to strengthening their Christologies, using "we" rather than "I" statements also helps connect teens with the saints who have gone before them; with the broader Christian tradition that anchors their faith. As Scot McKnight says:

> We dare not ignore what God has said to the church through the ages ... nor dare we fossilize past interpretations into traditionalism ... Reading the Bible *with* the Tradition gives us guidance but it also gives us freedom to differ with Tradition.[11]

In this way emphasizing their communal faith identity gives teens accountability, both for what they believe as well as for how they live.

HOST INTERFAITH DIALOGUES

To further help teens understand that Jesus is at the heart of the Christian faith, host interfaith dialogues. Now, before you disregard this idea as too dangerous, let me remind you that thanks to globalization, these conversations are already happening. The only question is whether or not we, as a church, will get to take part in them.

With that in mind, the next time you travel abroad for your summer mission trip, include an interfaith experience into your plans—not as an opportunity for evangelism, but rather as an opportunity to learn about the religion, culture, and customs of the people you're serving.

Closer to home, arrange a religious exchange. Go visit a local mosque or synagogue, and then invite the youth from there to visit your church.

Several years ago, my teens and I visited a Jewish synagogue for a Shabbat service. Afterward, we experienced the hospitality of this congregation as we joined their teens for an informal question-and-answer session. Teens from my congregation asked Jewish teens questions about what they believe and why (as well as how) their faith impacted their daily lives. Then Jewish teens reciprocated and asked my teens questions about their faith. Such an experience taught my group how to appreciate, value, and even learn from another faith tradition. At the same time, it gave them an opportunity to articulate the basics of their faith, something that's important not only for evangelism, but for their own faith formation (which we'll talk more about in chapter 9).

Alternatively, partner with a local mosque or synagogue to jointly serve within your community. Doing so benefits teens in several ways. According to Len Kageler, serving with those of other faiths connects teens "with the heart of God in helping the hurting." Perhaps more importantly, he goes on to say that working alongside those of other faiths also causes Christian young people to ask questions of their faith they may not have asked otherwise. According to Kageler, it's better for our youth to wonder about such things now, rather than after they've left home.[12]

Regardless of whether an interfaith dialogue or experience

takes place halfway around the world or right in your own backyard, take time to process it with teens. Because of how much emphasis our culture places on tolerance, simply teaching teens how to appreciate, value, and even learn from other faith traditions is no longer enough. Instead, take time to specifically ask teens to compare their faith with the faith tradition they just experienced.

Almost always, teens will begin by telling you what was similar about the two faiths. Affirm and acknowledge similarities. However, push deeper. Ask teens to name what's different between their faith and the one they just experienced. Explain that it's possible to name and discuss differences while still being respectful of people and their beliefs. Ensure your own tone and language models this to teens. Rather than foster doubt, acknowledging the differences between the Christian faith and other faith traditions gives teens ownership and confidence in their faith. It also gives teens the courage to confidently name Jesus as that which differentiates Christianity from all other world religions.

EXPLORE THE TRICKY PARTS OF SCRIPTURE

Since nearly one-quarter of the young people I surveyed didn't know if you could be a Christian without believing in Jesus, in order to strengthen this aspect of teens' Christologies, you need to take the time to specifically address this gap.
One way to do this is to take a break from your regular teaching and use your youth gatherings to read and discuss a book like Lee Strobel's *The Case for Christ: Student Edition*.[13] Such books not only give teens thoughtful responses to their honest questions, but—through their very existence—show teens they're not alone in the questions they're asking.

Explore some of the tricky, exclusivist passages in Scripture. Read and study Jesus' words to his disciples in John 14:6-7a, "I am the way and the truth and the life. No one comes to the

Father except through me. If you really know me, you will know my Father as well." Ask questions that invite your group to wrestle with what these words mean. What does it mean that no one comes to the Father except through Jesus? What do Jesus' own words suggest about his importance to the Christian faith?

As you explore these tricky questions, be prepared to tackle others that will likely arise. Examples include: *What happens to my friends and family members who don't believe in Jesus?* and *If God's so loving, how can he send people to hell?*

Regardless of how you personally would answer these questions, instead of presenting young people with only one answer, consider sharing multiple Christian perspectives, much in the same way we discussed teaching multiple atonement theories in chapter 4. For example, share all three of the following widely held, biblical, yet vastly different responses to these questions with your group (as framed and defined in the book *What About Those Who Have Never Heard?* by Gabriel Fackre, Roald Nash, and John Sanders):

Inclusivism: "The unevangelized may be saved if they respond in faith to God based on the revelation they have."

Divine Perseverance: "The unevangelized receive an opportunity to believe in Jesus after death."
Restrictivism: "God does not provide salvation to those who fail to hear of Jesus and come to faith in him before they die."[14]

EXPLAIN CHRISTIAN UNIVERSALISM

Recently when my youth ministry discussed what happens to those who haven't heard the gospel, one of the girls shared her vision of hell. According to her, hell is a jail complete with individual cells that have bars covering the door and microscopic windows. What's unusual about this young person's picture of hell is that the jail cells are empty. When you ask her why, she'll tell you she thinks it's because Jesus' death paid it *all*. According to her, Jesus' love is so strong that even hell can't separate people from it.

At school, this girl is regularly ridiculed for her belief. Her Christian friends tell her she's wrong. They tell her hell is a real place and that, as a result of her crazy beliefs about it, if she's not careful, she might end up there too.

Not long ago, I would have told her the same thing.

However, as a result of my research and my growing understanding of how to help teens conclude for themselves that Jesus is the only way to heaven, my response to her has recently changed. Nowadays, I affirm this young person's belief. I tell her that throughout history, lots of other Christians have agreed with her. Then I give her "crazy" belief a name: Christian universalism. In *What About Those Who've Never Heard?* Christian universalism is described as the belief that "all people will in fact be saved by Jesus. No one is damned forever."[15] It's the idea that one day hell will indeed be empty, just as this girl's vision suggests.

Then, together with everyone else in my youth ministry, we look at some of the Scripture passages that support this belief, including Romans 5:18, "Consequently, just as one trespass resulted in condemnation for all people, so also one righteous act resulted in justification and life for all people."

Finally, we distinguish between Christian universalism (what my student believes) and regular universalism (a widely held belief in today's tolerance-obsessed culture). Unlike Christian universalism, in regular universalism Jesus is nowhere to be found. According to regular or general universalism, everyone goes to heaven regardless of in whom (or what) they believe.

The difference is, no doubt, subtle. To be clear, it's easy for people—especially teens—to confuse the two. And given how unpopular Christian universalism is in many Christian circles, unless we intentionally distinguish between it and regular universalism, I fear it'll become far too easy for our young people to adhere to the latter and simply forget (or even deny) Jesus' role in salvation.

That, in a nutshell, is why my approach to this young girl has changed. I want her—and others like her—to understand the difference between these two belief systems. I hope she will continue to freely share her vision of hell with people. After all, it's an appealing one. By helping her see its place in Christendom, my hope is that she won't ever forget Jesus' role in emptying hell; that just as she does in my youth ministry, she'll boldly and confidently proclaim that hell may be empty, but that it's empty because of Jesus.

COEXIST WITH OTHER VIEWPOINTS

Just as I want those in my youth ministry who believe in Christian universalism to boldly and confidently proclaim that hell is empty because of Jesus, I want those who hold to a restrictivist viewpoint to feel equally confident in sharing their view of the atonement. Since those with restrictivist viewpoints are often called intolerant by both their Christian and non-Christian peers, helping them to confidently share their views first requires that we acknowledge how hurtful these labels are to adolescents.

Knowing this, applaud young people for their courage in sharing their faith with their friends. Together, wrestle with 1 Peter 3:15, "But in your hearts revere Christ as Lord. Always be prepared to give an answer to everyone who asks you to give the reason for the hope that you have. But do this with gentleness and respect." Challenge young people to consider how they can share their faith with people in a way that pushes them toward (rather than away from) Jesus. Help your group understand how they can be true to their beliefs and still be respectful of others.

FINAL THOUGHTS

I'm blessed to be part of a congregation that values interfaith dialogue and works together with people of all faiths for the betterment of our community. Shortly after the fighting in Syria began in 2011, members of a mosque with whom we've worked on several occasions contacted my congregation to see if we'd be willing to allow some of their parishioners to join us for worship. They wanted to tell us about the violence in Syria and ask our congregation to pray for peace.

We agreed. A few days later, Muslim youth and their families joined us for worship. They shared how the escalating conflict and civil war was impacting their family members who remained in Syria. Together, we prayed for peace in Syria. Afterward, teens from my youth ministry invited the visiting youth to join us for Sunday school. (At the time, we were actually in the midst of a series about Jesus prompted by the small-scale research project I'd done for my christological foundations class—the one that set this whole study in motion.)

That morning, a dozen or so Muslim young people joined those from my youth ministry for an engaging discussion about Jesus. Together, we dove into Scripture (the Gospels in particular) and explored some of what Jesus did and said. Together, we wrestled with some of the biggest questions of the Christian faith, including two we've explored in this book: whether or not Jesus was God, and whether or not he was perfect. The youth certainly disagreed with one another, yet everyone—even our Muslim guests—felt welcome enough to share their honest responses to these questions.

I'm pretty sure we didn't convert anyone that day.

Yet, I'm equally sure my group and I encountered Jesus. Forced to take a look at their faith with fresh eyes and to respond to honest questions from their peers, the young people in my youth ministry began to see Jesus—and his centrality to the Christian faith—in a new light. I watched as they began to claim him as the distinctive of our Christian faith.

That day, teens in my youth ministry began to understand that you cannot be a Christian without Jesus.

Beyond that, however, they left understanding that far from making us intolerant, our belief in Jesus actually compels us to welcome and love *all* people.

CHAPTER NOTES

1. Teaching Tolerance, "What Is Mix It Up at Lunch Day?" *Teaching Tolerance: A Project of the Southern Poverty Law Center,* www.tolerance.org/mix-it-up/what-is-mix.

2. Mike Nappa, *The Jesus Survey: What Christian Teens Really Believe and Why* (Grand Rapids, MI: Baker Books, 2012), 77.

3. Thom S. Rainer and Jess W. Rainer, *The Millennials: Connecting to America's Largest Generation* (Nashville: B&H Publishing Group, 2011), 233.

4. David Kinnaman, *You Lost Me: Why Young Christians Are Leaving Church and Rethinking Faith* (Grand Rapids, MI: Baker Books, 2011), 176.

5. Robert D. Putnam and David E. Campbell, *American Grace: How Religion Divides and Unites Us* (New York: Simon & Schuster, 2010), 536.

6. Greg L. Hawkins and Cally Parkinson, *Move: What 1,000 Churches Reveal About Spiritual Growth* (Grand Rapids, MI: Zondervan, 2011), 31.

7. Rainer and Rainer, *The Millennials*, 228.

8. Hawkins and Parkinson, *Move*, 12, 36.

9. Len Kageler, *Youth Ministry in a Multifaith Society: Forming Christian Identity Among Skeptics, Syncretists and Sincere Believers of Other Faiths* (Downers Grove, IL: InterVarsity Press, 2014), 134–135.

10. Nappa, *The Jesus Survey*, 73.

11. Scot McKnight, *The Blue Parakeet: Rethinking How You Read the Bible* (Grand Rapids, MI: Zondervan, 2008), 34.

12. Kageler, *Youth Ministry in a Multifaith Society*, 147.

13. Lee Strobel with Jane Vogel. *The Case for Christ: Student Edition* (Grand Rapids, MI: Zondervan/Youth Specialties, 2001).

14. Gabriel Fackre, Roald H. Nash, and John Sanders. *What About Those Who Have Never Heard? Three Views on the Destiny of the Unevangelized* (Downers Grove, IL: InterVarsity Press, 1995), 20.

15. Ibid.

CHAPTER 6

JESUS: THE WORLD'S GREATEST TEACHER

Between my sophomore and junior years of college, I worked for YouthWorks Missions, an organization that exists to connect teenagers to God, each other, and communities, through life-changing Christ-centered mission trips. That summer, our theme was "Be Like Jesus." As a staff member, I spent the entire summer trying to figure out what this meant in my own life and then helping high school teens to do the same.

As part of our exploration of this, at the beginning of each week, I'd ask the youth to write their names on small pieces of paper. Then, each day we'd draw several of the names. We'd spend a few minutes sharing specific ways we'd seen each of those people be like Jesus.

"She was like Jesus when she loved that little boy."

"I saw Jesus in him when he hung out with Sammie, even though I knew he'd rather have been playing kickball."

"He was like Jesus when he kept playing with her, despite how frustrating she was today."

"I saw Jesus in her when she encouraged her buddy to sing."

Through this activity, it became clear that to teens, being like Jesus means emulating him and following his example, which means obeying his teachings—something we cannot do unless we know what Jesus taught. But do teens actually know what Jesus taught?

WHAT DID JESUS TEACH?

To find out, on the surveys I used a short-answer question to ask young people what Jesus taught. More than one-quarter of the respondents (28 percent) said Jesus taught "love"—both God's love for us, as well as the fact that we're called to love others. At first glance, this might appear to be an easy, churchy answer. But it's also a very biblical one. As one participant reminded me, "Jesus gave us the two most important commandments: 'Love the Lord your God with all your heart, and with all your soul, and with all your mind, and with all your strength. Love your neighbor as yourself.' I think that's like the summary of everything that he taught."

The next two most frequent responses to this question were that Jesus taught "the Word of God" and that he taught "about God"—each of which were said by 14 percent of the young people. After this came "forgiveness" (9 percent) and "how to live" (7 percent).

TEACHER CLASSIFICATIONS

Since many of the responses to this question were said infrequently, to better understand them I did a second type of analysis in which I disregarded frequency and, instead, grouped similar responses into unique categories. I then gave each category a heading describing which facet of Jesus' teaching it represented. As with the Jesus archetypes found in chapter 1, these labels are not all-encompassing. All contain elements of truth, but several also reflect the adolescents' mistaken assumptions about what Jesus taught.

JESUS: A RELIGIOUS TEACHER

Analyzing the participants' responses in this way revealed that approximately one-third (36 percent) of the adolescents mentioned things they believed Jesus taught in accordance with faith. Responses categorized as faith-related indicate

Jesus taught the basics of Christianity, including God, the Holy Spirit, discipleship, grace, hope, salvation, and heaven. He also taught Scripture. In particular, he taught the Old Testament, including the Ten Commandments. Additionally, respondents mentioned that Jesus said things that later became Scripture, like parables and the Sermon on the Mount. Jesus also modeled basic Christian disciplines such as prayer, service, and worship. These types of responses show that youth see Jesus as a religious teacher.

JESUS: A SELF-HELP GURU

Approximately one-fifth (19 percent) of participants' responses were categorized as self-help. These included things like the belief that Jesus taught ...

"You are able."
"You're special."
"Do your best."
"Be good."
"Never give up."
"Be smart."
"Smile."
"Life goes on."
"Don't worry."

These responses indicate that this group of youth sees Jesus as a self-help guru—not unlike Dr. Phil—who's capable of helping them achieve their dreams. Interestingly, the stronger an adolescent's Christology, the less frequently his responses fell into the self-help category.

JESUS: A SOCIAL ACTIVIST

Another way young people see Jesus is as a social activist, someone whose life and teaching models social justice, as well as how to live in community with others. Responses to the question of what Jesus taught were categorized in this way with 18 percent of those surveyed. They include things like Jesus taught us to accept others, be compassionate, break down walls, and work toward peace and reconciliation.

JESUS: A MORAL TEACHER

Yet another way young people see Jesus is as a moral teacher. Given the prevalence of morality teachings in many Christian circles, I expected this category to be huge. In reality, only 6 percent of the teens' responses fit into it. Responses classified in this category show that Jesus taught morals, good from bad, and right versus wrong. He also taught us not to sin.

JESUS: OUR FOUNDING FATHER

An additional 6 percent of youth responses were categorized as American ideals. Responses that fell into this category depict Jesus teaching things like equality, ethics, fairness, freedom of religion, liberty, and tolerance. These responses indicate our young people see Jesus as one of America's Founding Fathers.

THINGS JESUS DIDN'T REALLY TEACH: "RELIGION"

Unfortunately, some of what young people think Jesus taught is simply inaccurate. Take, for example, the picture some adolescents have of Jesus as a Founding Father. Though this picture as a whole isn't entirely inaccurate, some of its specifics certainly are. Rather than teaching freedom of religion, Jesus taught that he is the way, the truth, and the life; that if you know him, you'll also know God (John 14:6-7). As we discussed in chapter 5, he also taught love, not tolerance.

According to Jesus' own words, he came not to abolish but rather to fulfill the law (Matthew 5:17). Even so, while Jesus modeled a variety of Christian practices, another thing he didn't teach was "religion," at least not as we've commonly come to think of it today. For Jesus, religion seemed to include not just beliefs or a list of do's and don'ts, but rather a call to proclaim "the good news of the kingdom" and heal "every disease and sickness among the people" (Matthew 4:23). Such an understanding of religion actually clashed greatly with the day's religious establishment.

Likewise, Jesus didn't teach "Christianity," *per se*. While what we've come to call Christianity is certainly centered on Christ, it began only after Jesus' death and resurrection. As one student said, Jesus didn't "start a religion, his followers did." In the same way, even though much of what Jesus taught can be found in the New Testament, Jesus couldn't have actually taught *from* the New Testament. Its contents were written years after his resurrection and canonized even later.

THINGS JESUS DIDN'T REALLY TEACH: "IT'S OKAY TO SIN"

Another false impression teens have is that Jesus taught it's okay to sin. Though Jesus taught grace and forgiveness, not once did he say sinning was okay. Consider, for a moment, the story of the adulterous woman in John 8. After a woman accused of adultery is brought before him, Jesus tells the Pharisees that if any of them is without sin, they can throw the first stone. Knowing they too have sinned, the Pharisees leave. Jesus then offers this woman extravagant love and grace but tells her, "Go now and leave your life of sin," confident her encounter with him will change her.

THINGS JESUS DIDN'T REALLY TEACH: "GOOD DEEDS WILL SAVE YOU"

Teens also mistakenly believe salvation is earned through works, not grace. To be clear, Jesus undoubtedly modeled servant leadership to his followers. He met people's spiritual needs as well as their physical ones, not only offering them forgiveness, but often feeding and healing them as well. He also told parables—like the one about the sheep and the goats in Matthew 25—that emphasized the importance of meeting people's needs. I don't see him suggesting, however, that any of these deeds would save people, thereby teaching salvation through works. Instead, Jesus connected our actions with our love for him, saying in John 14:23, "Anyone who loves me will obey my teaching. My Father will love them, and we will come to them and make our home with them." In other words, we serve not to earn God's love but to respond to it.

CORRECT MISCONCEPTIONS

To strengthen young people's understanding of what Jesus taught, begin by correcting their misconceptions. As we discussed in chapter 3, dig into Scripture and, in particular, Jesus' words in the Gospels. Unless teens read what Jesus actually taught, they assume he taught the same things other good teachers taught. In essence, this reduces Jesus to a civics teacher concerned with the welfare of a community, but not necessarily the faith of a community.

To further strengthen teens' understanding of what Jesus taught, do a series about "Stuff Jesus Didn't Say." Address the aforementioned misconceptions about what young people believe Jesus taught. Add to this list two more other popular misconceptions: happiness and fairness. American culture is currently hyper-obsessed with both.

Additionally, be prepared to confront these misconceptions whenever they show up in your conversations with youth or their parents. For example, I recently read a testimony from one of my young people, written in preparation for an upcoming mission trip. In it, he repeatedly talked about how Jesus wanted him to be happy.

My response to this was greatly shaped by my research and, in particular, by knowing how confused adolescents often are about what Jesus actually taught. Rather than ignore or immediately refute his statement, I asked him why he thought this way. After hearing his explanation, I asked him to show me where in Scripture Jesus said he wants us to be happy. This young man thought about this for several minutes before saying, "Well, maybe he didn't. But my parents want me to be happy, so I guess I always thought Jesus did too."

I then gently pushed back. I reminded him how deeply Jesus does, in fact, care about us. Together, we read Matthew 16:24, "Then Jesus said to his disciples, 'Whoever wants to be my disciple must deny themselves and take up their cross and follow me.' " We then discussed whether or not this passage (and others like it) support the idea that Jesus' ultimate concern is our happiness. Doing so prompted some good, honest conversation. More importantly, through it, I watched this young person's understanding of Jesus deepen.

Do the same thing whenever you hear your youth attribute something to Jesus that he didn't say. Ask young people to explain why they believe what they do. Then call out their misconceptions. Together, dig into Scripture passages that correct faulty understanding. As you do, ask questions that will help teens better understand what Jesus really taught.

Similarly, when teens correctly attribute something to Jesus, play devil's advocate by pushing back. Regularly ask the question: *Where in Scripture did Jesus say that?* So many of teens' misconceptions about what Jesus taught stem from biblical illiteracy. So help them connect the dots. Rather than assuming teens know where in Scripture they can find things (like the Golden Rule), ask them to actually find it. If they can't, don't shame or belittle them. Instead, introduce them to online resources like *BibleGateway.com.* Show them how to search for keywords and find what they're looking for in Scripture. As they learn what Jesus actually said and where in Scripture those teachings are found, teens' confidence will increase and so will their ability to take ownership of their faith.

TEACH CHURCH HISTORY

Another way to correct teens' misconceptions about what
Jesus taught is to teach church history, particularly that of the
early church. My experience has traditionally been that when
mainline churches tackle church history, they do so from a
denominational perspective, largely ignoring the history of the
greater church as a whole. On the other hand, the evangelical
churches I've attended have, for the most part, ignored
anything beyond early church history. Maybe that's why
many young people's misconceptions about what Jesus taught
surround our broader early church history and, in particular, its
timeline.

To remedy this, teach early church history to teens with
a particular focus on the apostolic age and events that are
recorded within the book of Acts. Don't get caught up in
the minutiae, but as you teach throughout the year, create
a timeline. Place each story you teach on the timeline so
young people begin to understand when events happened
in relationship to one another. Include major events in the
story of our faith on this timeline, including Jesus' death,
resurrection, and the coming of the Holy Spirit at Pentecost. As
you introduce new stories, talk about when that particular book
of the Bible was written and add that to your timeline as well.
Also add things like when the Bible was canonized. Doing so
will help your group understand not only the basics of church
history (including what Jesus taught and when), but also their
place in God's unfolding story.

BUILD ON WHAT THEY ALREADY KNOW

In addition to correcting misconceptions about what Jesus
taught, it's equally important to celebrate and build upon what
teens already know. According to my research, what teens
know is that Jesus taught love—both God's love for us and
the importance of loving others. So wrestle with what God's

love looks like by studying the person of Jesus. Help teens understand that to know what God's love looks like, they have to look no further than the person of Jesus. As New Testament scholar N. T. Wright says, "Jesus is the mirror-image of the God who is there but who we normally can't see."[1] With that in mind, explore Jesus' life and the myriad of ways he showed God's love for others in his interactions with people of all kinds.

As a part of this, talk specifically about how much Jesus loves individual people. Now, I understand that for some, this might be a tough pill to swallow given how often in our society individualism seems to trump community. For this reason, it's tempting to celebrate young people who talk about Jesus' love for everyone. After all, John 3:16 says, "For God so loved the *world* ..."

Recently, however, I had a conversation with a teen that made me reinterpret this kind of response. The conversation was sparked by our discussion about Jefferson Bethke's book, *Jesus > Religion*. In the first chapter, Jefferson shares: "We've lost the real Jesus—or at least exchanged him for a newer, safer, sanitized, ineffectual one."[2] Since this young person was captivated by this idea, we spent time comparing and contrasting "fake Jesus" with the "real Jesus." In distinguishing between the two, she remarked, "The fake Jesus loves everyone. The real Jesus loves you ... as an individual. He knows you personally."

Concerned that her "real Jesus" might be a bit too individualistic, I asked her to elaborate. She explained how it's easy to say Jesus loves everyone. According to her, that's what you have to say in our society today. It's much harder to say (and grasp) that Jesus loves *you*—regardless of your quirks or sins. Building upon what our young people know about Jesus' love requires us to take a both/and approach that emphasizes the breadth and depth of his love, as well as the love he has for each one of his unique creations.

As you wrestle with Jesus' love, another thing to keep in mind is that teens often equate it with the type of love they've experienced from their parents. For some teens, this means God's love is far from the type of "perfect love that drives out fear" described in 1 John 4:18. Instead, it's actually riddled with fear. Sometimes young people with this kind of background believe the second they screw up, God will stop loving them. So teach often that *this* is the Good News of the gospel of Jesus: God's love for us is so great that Jesus died for us while we were still sinners (Romans 5:8).

ACKNOWLEDGE SIN

Since Jesus died for us while we were *still* sinners, it's important to acknowledge sin with teens. We all screw up. We all sin, despite our best efforts not to. Knowing this, I want teens to know that when—not if—they mess up, Jesus will still love them. At the same time, I want young people to understand that sin is wrong; it separates us from both God and each other.

To be honest, it greatly disturbed me to hear teens say that Jesus taught it's okay to sin. Their responses immediately made me question why this is. Is this a result of a culture wherein everything is okay? Is this because American society is obsessed with building up teens' self-esteem, so much so that we fear that if we tell a teen she did something wrong, it'll destroy her self-worth and her future? Or is this because we've stopped talking about sin—even within the church? After all, it's not very welcoming to talk about sin.

In my own ministry, I confess that I rarely talk about sin. I don't want to scar my youth in the same way I've been scarred by communities that defined accountability as the practice of recounting how awful we are, out loud to one another, day in and day out. Rather than help me focus on Jesus, such practices made me focus on my sin instead. They left me feeling ashamed, further separated from God, and convinced that even his love couldn't overcome my awfulness.

I'll be the first to say I don't want my youth to feel that way.

But I do want them to know the God who is revealed through Jesus and through Scripture. And like it or not, 1 John 1:9 says, "If we confess our sins, he is faithful and just and will forgive us our sins and purify us from all unrighteousness."

A few years ago, my student leaders and I read and discussed *Relearning Jesus* by Matthew Paul Turner. One of the chapters in this book ("The Heart Part") deals with the importance of confession. In it, Turner explains:

> Purity gives me a chance when I am weak enough to be completely honest with my friend. Purity comes when I know that this story I am living is not about me—when I live out the truth that my story is about being a part of Jesus' story.[3]

This idea greatly challenged my young people, who didn't like being told the story they're living isn't actually about them and who couldn't understand how purity might invite honesty.

So we decided to practice. Over the next several weeks, we committed to pay attention to the confession our congregation says during worship and then to report what we noticed.

Truthfully, I was amazed at what my group noticed. They talked about how—as a result of being challenged by our discussion—they actually confessed their sins during the silence for personal confession, rather than simply zoning out. They spoke of the freedom they experienced from that simple act. Some spoke about how differently they experienced Communion when they actively engaged in confession. Still others talked about confessing something regarding another person—a relationship issue—and then sharing the peace of the Lord with that same person later on during the worship service and experiencing release.

Hearing those stories made me—and them—realize that confession is, in fact, an important spiritual practice. It grants us freedom and the peace that passes all understanding. At the same time, it fosters the kind of deep, rich community that's an important catalyst for spiritual growth.

So let's acknowledge and name sin through confession.

But let's also practice grace.

PRACTICE GRACE

The thing that most surprised me about participants' responses to the question of what Jesus taught is that a few said Jesus taught works, not grace—an idea that runs contrary to 500 years of protestant teaching. Once again, seeing and hearing responses like these made me question their origin.
I began wondering if our actions contradict our teaching about grace. As a result of what we say and how we act, do young people look at those on our elder boards and assume they're better Christians than those who are not? Do requirements for baptism and confirmation also contribute to this belief?

Now, I'm a big believer in setting high expectations for the youth with whom we work (as you'll see in chapter 7 when we discuss the importance of raising the bar). That said, even in my church's relatively low-key confirmation ministry, teens are still required to attend class on a weekly basis and complete a certain number of sermon notes during each of the two years they're in confirmation. Might it be possible that such requirements communicate to teens that just as they have to complete certain requirements in order to become members of our churches, they must also earn their salvation?

From 2007 to 2010, Kara Powell oversaw the College Transition Project for Fuller Youth Institute. The study's fascinating findings are described in *Sticky Faith, Youth Worker Edition*—authored by Powell, Brad Griffin, and Cheryl Crawford—and they suggest we're inadvertently passing on a faith that must be earned. According to their research: "Many of us have been taught, or at least modeled (usually unintentionally), that freedom doesn't actually mean freedom, but rather switching from one form of bondage (sin) to another (the gospel of 'sin management')." Such an approach fosters faith in teens that, according to the *Sticky Faith* authors, isn't "large enough to handle those inevitable mistakes."[4]

For teens to understand that Jesus showed and taught grace, they have to experience it in their own lives. This requires us to explain it—and the best way to explain it is to show tangible expressions of it. Grace needs to be our default position, the way in which we reflexively respond to young people. Teens experience grace when we encourage them to try new things, rather than force them to compete against one another for positions of honor. They also experience grace when we help them learn from their mistakes.

During my rookie year in youth ministry, I had an exceptionally hard time showing grace to my group. To me, their faith seemed lackadaisical. It appeared what they needed most was not grace, but a kick in the pants, which I was all too willing to give them.

Throughout that year I struggled in particular with one individual in the group. She did everything those of us who are evangelicals like to rail against: She was sexually active, smoke, and drank. On multiple occasions, I kicked her out of youth group. I did so even though I knew she came from a difficult home. In fact, I knew she lived with an extended family member because her mom was in jail.

To this day, the way I treated this girl haunts me.

I wonder what a difference I—and more importantly, Jesus—might have made in her life if rather than coming down on the side of the law, I'd shown her grace.

Having had ample time to reflect on that experience, now I always try to err on the side of grace. I don't always get this right, but on those rare occasions when I do, I'm reminded of how powerfully grace expresses Jesus' love to us.

For example, I once took a mission trip during which people's air mattresses repeatedly malfunctioned. We'd leave for the day and return to our room to find another one completely deflated. We scoured the floor on our hands and knees, searching for a sharp object capable of destroying air mattress after air mattress. We found none.

After the same thing happened on several days, I finally concluded vandalism was at fault. Eventually, someone handed me a pushpin and gave me the name of the youth responsible for deliberately destroying people's air mattresses.

In that moment, I was mad. Thanks to this teenager, I was also sleeping on the cold, hard floor as my ruined air mattress laid in a heap next to me, as if taunting me.

My immediate reaction was to send her home.

Instead, I gave myself time to calm down before confronting

her. I thought and prayed through the situation, and as I did, I saw the face of that girl from my rookie year in ministry. In that moment, I knew I had to respond not with punishment, but with grace. So I confronted her with the offending pin in hand. When I asked why she'd done it, tears gushed from this normally stoic girl's face. She shared about the pressure and expectations she faced at home and how she felt as though she never did anything right.

Though the rules suggested punishment, grace compelled me to do otherwise. So I hugged her, forgave her, laid out the consequences of her behavior (apologies, a conversation with her parents, and the purchase of new air mattresses for all involved), told her how important she was to our group, and then gave her another chance. In that moment, this young person encountered Jesus. I know this is true because I saw a tangible difference in her behavior and attitude that outlasted the trip.

BE LIKE JESUS

As I've grown older, I've become more and more convinced that it takes a lifetime to figure out what it means to be like Jesus. Truthfully, I'm not even sure that at the end of my life I'll be able to say with certainty: "This is what it means to be like Jesus."

What I do know is that I want "be like Jesus" to be more than a cutesy phrase I use with my youth ministry. I want it to be something that challenges them to actually live like Jesus. And that can't happen unless they know Jesus—who he is, what he did, why he died, and what he taught.

CHAPTER NOTES

1. N. T. Wright, *Paul for Everyone: The Prison Letters* (London: Society for Promoting Christian Knowledge, 2002), 151.
2. Jefferson Bethke, *Jesus > Religion: Why He Is So Much Better Than Trying Harder, Doing More, and Being Good Enough* (Nashville: Thomas Nelson Books, 2013), 9.
3. Matthew Paul Turner, *Relearning Jesus: How Reading the Beatitudes One More Time Changed My Faith* (Colorado Springs: David C. Cook, 2009), 80.
4. Kara E. Powell, Brad M. Griffin, and Cheryl A. Crawford, *Sticky Faith, Youth Worker Edition: Practical Ideas to Nurture Long-Term Faith in Teenagers* (Grand Rapids, MI: Zondervan/Youth Specialties, 2011), 33, 43.

SECTION 2
KEYS FOR STRENGTHENING THE CHRISTOLOGY OF TEENS

CHAPTER 7

PRIORITIZE FAITH

Once every three years, I use the word *required* to describe just one type of youth ministry event: monthly mission trip meetings designed to prepare a mission team for its international experience.

Team members know about these meetings from the get-go. They even sign and return a covenant detailing this requirement along with their application. Yet, inevitably, this requirement creates problems when something else—typically a sporting event—conflicts with it. Parents will then contact me and explain how their child will not be able to attend the meeting. They do so, fully expecting that I'll allow their child to miss the agreed-upon meeting. When I don't, they get upset.

After 12 years in ministry, these reactions should no longer surprise me, especially since I know that in recent years, the church has lost much of its influence and standing. In contrast to the 1950s and 1960s, the church is no longer the center of American society. It is, at best, one of many other extracurricular activities that vie for our families' time.

THE IMPORTANCE OF FAITH TO TEENS

Despite the battles church workers often wage with church families over their time and priorities, many teens say faith is important to them. In fact, over half of the young people I surveyed (57 percent) said their faith was very important to them. An additional 37 percent said it was somewhat important to them.

When asked specifically about the importance of Jesus to their faith, the majority of those I surveyed (67 percent) said Jesus was very important to their faith. An additional 25 percent said Jesus was somewhat important to their faith.

Since the young people I surveyed were all active in their congregations, I expected these numbers to be high, but I didn't honestly expect them to be that high. In light of my experience with church families, numbers this high simply don't make sense to me. If teens value their faith and the role of Jesus in their faith, shouldn't they also prioritize church?

CHRISTOLOGY SCORES

In order to dig deeper into this phenomenon, I created a tool—the Christology Score—to measure the strength of teens' Christologies and then compare them to other phenomenon, like the importance of faith. Christology Scores were based on young people's answers to the seven multiple-choice Christology questions found on the survey (which we discussed in chapters 2 through 6). Participants received one point for each correct answer and no points for incorrect answers or responses of "I don't know." The higher the score, the more Christology questions they answered in accordance with the orthodox Christian understanding of them. The highest score, a seven, indicated they answered all seven Christology questions correct. Conversely, a score of zero meant the participants got none of the Christology questions correct.

Only 54 percent of all the young people surveyed got more than half of the Christology questions correct—an astounding number, considering those I surveyed were active in their congregations. More specifically, only 9 percent achieved a perfect Christology Score of seven, while 11 percent received a score of six; 17 percent received a score of five and four; 30 percent received a score of three; 15 percent received a score of two; and 1 percent received a score of one and zero. (See Figure 9.)

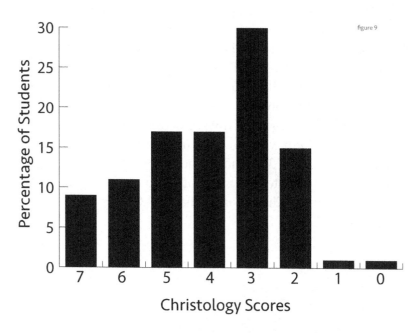

figure 9

AVERAGE CHRISTOLOGY SCORES

The overall average Christology Score for all 369 young
people surveyed was a 4.0. Two of the church sites I visited had
average Christology Scores that were greater than that. Youth
from the Bible Belt congregation had the highest average
Christology Score of 5.67. The small-town congregation I
visited had the next highest average score of 4.63—more than
a full point lower than that of the Bible Belt congregation, but
still well above the overall average Christology Score. The
remaining two sites had average Christology Scores that fell
below the overall average. The average Christology Score
for the suburban congregation was a 3.74, while the rural
congregation had the lowest average Christology Score with a
3.6.

To enable me to begin exploring various relationships in
the data, I also calculated average Christology Scores for
each subset of young people who ranked the importance of

their faith in a particular way. Doing so revealed that the more important faith was to adolescents, the stronger their Christologies. Only those who said faith was "very important" to them had an average Christology Score (4.37) that was higher than the overall average Christology Score of 4.0. (See Figure 10.) Those who said faith was "somewhat important" to them had an average Christology Score of 3.61, while those who said faith was "not very important" had an average Christology Score of 3.0. Those who said faith was "irrelevant" had an average Christology Score of 1.8, a number well below the overall average Christology Score of 4.0.

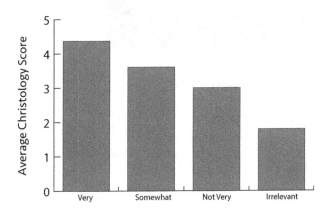

figure 10

This trend also held true for the relationship between Christology Scores and the importance of Jesus to the faith of teens. Teens who ranked Jesus as very important to their faith had average Christology Scores that were much higher (4.32) than those who said Jesus was irrelevant (0.83).

This makes a great deal of sense. Just consider the old adage: You make time for what's important to you. If that's true, then teens who say their faith is important to them make time for it. As a result, they grow in their faith and their Christologies are strengthened. In the same way, if teens say Jesus is important to their faith, they will make time for him. As a result, they will

132

grow in their relationships with him and their Christologies will, once again, be strengthened.

This, of course, raises an important question: If the strength of young people's Christologies are related to how important their faith is to them, then how can we help teens prioritize their faith—especially in a culture in which faith (and church) are no longer central?

COUNT THE COST

To begin, we must recognize the truth that author Jon Huckins (with Rob Yackley) offers in the book *Thin Places*: "A vast number of Christians in the West are terribly bored ... Our faith has become so domesticated that followers of Jesus really don't know what it means to follow Jesus."[1] Given this, we need to shatter the myth that Jesus and faith are boring.

To be clear, the antidote to boredom is not entertainment. Years ago, Young Life Founder Jim Rayburn said, "It is a crime to bore anyone with the gospel."[2] Too often, however, I think those of us in ministry have interpreted this as: "It's our job to make the gospel interesting by entertaining teens." The truth is, the gospel is already interesting, and so is Jesus.

So instead of entertaining teens, help them prioritize their faith by engaging them in it. Get teens into Scripture and, more specifically, into the Gospels. Introduce them to the teachings of Jesus, to a faith worth dying for and a cause worth living for. Dissect Jesus' words to his disciples in Mark 8:34, "Whoever wants to be my disciple must deny themselves and take up their cross and follow me." Challenge teens to consider what cross Jesus might be calling them to pick up in order to follow him. Dare them to honestly contemplate the cost of doing so. Then, instead of highlighting those who make a halfhearted, lackadaisical commitment to Jesus and their faith, affirm those who carefully contemplate the cost of doing so and integrate their faith into other parts of their lives, outside of church.

In the same way, wrestle with Jesus' words in Matthew 10:34, "Do not suppose that I have come to bring peace to the earth. I did not come to bring peace, but a sword." Once again challenge teens to weigh the cost of following Jesus, knowing that doing so will demand sacrifices. Dispel the myth that following Jesus is easy by giving practical examples of how the way of Jesus is countercultural. Talk about the student who leads the environmental club at school because she believes her faith compels her to care for God's creation. Share about teens who befriend those on the margins of their schools or who serve at their local soup kitchens—even on those days when they'd rather not. Tell the story of the young person who, much to her family's horror, turned down a high-paying summer internship in order to work for a mission organization. As you share these examples, remind teens that following Jesus is sometimes hard, but it's always transformational. In all of this, be careful not to sell teens short. After all, as authors Kenda Creasy Dean and Ron Foster state in *The Godbearing Life*: "Youth are capable of ridiculous fidelity to a cause worthy of their total commitment."[3]

DISCERN VOCATION

As teens begin seeing and experiencing the transformational power of Jesus in their own lives, they'll prioritize both Jesus and their faith. One key to this is to help young people connect their faith with their daily lives.

So often, teens—especially those raised in the more evangelical world—view faith as something very "pie in the sky," as an insurance policy that very well may pay off after death, but has little, if any, impact on life now. To combat this, study Jesus' words in the Gospels. Explore John 10:10, in which Jesus says, "The thief comes only to steal and kill and destroy; I have come that they may have life, and have it to the full." Put those words back into their context. Then wrestle with what it means that Jesus came to give us life. Share with your teens how Jesus gives you life. Then ask them to do the same.

Likewise, explore Jesus' words in the Lord's Prayer: "Your kingdom come, your will be done, on earth as it is in heaven" (Matthew 6:10). Ask teens: *Why do we pray for God's kingdom to come here? How can you be a part of God's kingdom work today? This week? In five years?*

As you wrestle with these questions, ponder two specific things with teens: vocation and service. Vocation is, I believe, one of the most misunderstood concepts in the Christian faith. Too often we've used it synonymously either with career or God's will. When we confuse vocation with career, we risk trivializing both. Perhaps more dangerously, we risk assuming a person's career is always the same thing as his or her vocation. While that may be true in some instances, it's not always the case.

On the other hand, confusing vocation with God's will is perhaps even more dangerous. So often, searching for God's will leads to paralysis. Convinced God's will is one specific thing in our lives, we live in fear of missing it. Rather than risk doing something wrong, we settle for the status quo and do nothing at all.

What would happen if—rather than adding to the vocational confusion of teens—we instilled in them a different understanding of vocation? What would happen if we taught teens Frederick Buechner's definition of vocation as "the place where your deep gladness and the world's deep hunger meet"?[4]

Such an understanding of vocation would give teens a more concrete way of discerning the otherwise nebulous and abstract notion of call. It would give teens the freedom to try new things in order to discover their gifts and dream about how God might be calling them to use those gifts to serve and honor him. It would give young people permission to pay attention to their emotions, to acknowledge when something breaks their hearts, and to question how God might be at work through those emotions. Such a definition of vocation would also give them the opportunity to experience the pure, unadulterated joy that comes from living life at the intersection of their own gladness and the world's deep needs.

I know this because I've seen it play out in the lives of some of my young people. A few years ago, I had the privilege of taking a team from our youth group to Rwanda. There, we learned about forgiveness and reconciliation by visiting the genocide memorials. We rolled paper beads with HIV-positive women trying to earn a living wage for their families. We walked the path rural children take each day to fetch water. We stood at the top of a mountain in a refugee camp and looked across Lake Kivu and heard a Congolese man describe the beauty of a home he knew he'd never see again.

Such encounters simultaneously broke the hearts of my youth and ignited their passions. They began wrestling with what God might be calling them to do as a result of what they'd seen and experienced firsthand. In the process, their understanding of their vocations changed. One young person chose to study international relations in college because that's where his gladness and "the world's deep hunger" met. Another began a nonprofit called Countries Without Cavities after he saw firsthand how inadequate healthcare is in the refugee camps. After seeing how important milk is to rural families living in poverty, a third student reoriented her future toward working for Heifer International.

Still others were convicted to come back and serve immediately. One teen spent her sophomore year in high school mentoring a refugee family. Having experienced the hospitality of refugees in Rwanda, she returned to our community determined to extend hospitality to them. After learning about how refugee children have no opportunity for education in the refugee camps after grade nine, another young person became their advocate, even speaking to our local school board about the issue.

Still others returned home and began serving in a weekly Kids Club for refugee children. Over nine months' time, teens formed deep relationships with the children they served, helping them with homework, playing games, leading crafts, practicing reading, and feeding them healthy snacks. At the same time, these refugee children enriched and enlivened the faith of my youth. Their ongoing presence in the lives of my teens ensured that their faith—and, in particular, their acts of service—continued to be their priority.

DEEPEN COMMUNITY

As teens become more and more interconnected with others through service, inevitably they'll also begin to grasp the power of community—something that further helps them to prioritize both Jesus and their faith.

As teens taste the power of community, continue taking the time to deepen their understanding of it. Compare and contrast the legendary church of Acts 2:42-47 with your own community:

> They devoted themselves to the apostles' teaching and to fellowship, to the breaking of bread and to prayer. Everyone was filled with awe at the many wonders and signs performed by the apostles. All the believers were together and had everything in common. They sold property and possessions to give to anyone who had need. Every day they continued to meet together in the temple courts. They broke bread in their homes

and ate together with glad and sincere hearts, praising God and enjoying the favor of all the people. And the Lord added to their number daily those who were being saved.

Cast a vision for deep community by sharing the role it's played in your own life. For example, I often tell my teens about the small-group community that my husband and I were blessed to be a part of for many years. We talk a lot about all we went through with this group of people: job changes, moves, the birth of children, and even the death of spouses. We share how, over the course of meals, trips, and countless hours together, we laughed, cried, and prayed with this group. Because we valued one another greatly, we willingly made sacrifices for each other, weathered conflict, and endured. In the process, we encountered Jesus through each and every person in the group.

We also talk frequently about how even though this small group has stopped meeting regularly, some of the people from it are still our closest friends today. I willingly share this with teens because I know many of them have never tasted this kind of Christ-centered community. As a result, I want them to know how life-giving such a community is; that it's well worth seeking out and investing in.

After casting a vision for deep community, give teens the space to confess those times when they've settled for superficial community. Then challenge them to strive for deep community, the kind that is often hard to find, yet always transformational. Call out authentic, honest community wherever and whenever you find it, regardless of whether or not it's in the church.

Remind teens of the integral role they play in community. Help them understand that to be part of a community, they must be willing to be committed to and held accountable to it. Show them that community is about something bigger than each of them as individuals and that, as a result, they won't always get their way. Instead, there will be times when they'll have to set aside their own wants and desires for the good of the greater community.

To this end, hold teens accountable to the commitments they make to Jesus, their faith community, and their community at large. When teens agree to be somewhere, don't let them off the hook if and when something better comes their way. When teens agree to do something, take away their safety nets and let them know you're counting on them to actually deliver. (And when, not if, they occasionally fail, practice grace—just as we discussed in chapter 6.) Doing so combats narcissism. It takes the spotlight off teens' wants and desires and puts it back on the person whom their faith actually revolves around: Jesus.

INTEGRATE TEENS INTO THE BROADER COMMUNITY

As teens' understanding of community grows, break down the walls that separate them from your broader church community. Pointing back to *Sticky Faith, Youth Worker Edition*, the College Transition Project found: "Involvement in all-church worship during high school is more consistently linked with mature faith in both high school and college than any other form of church participation."[5] It's often in intergenerational worship services that teens first form relationships with people who've been living out and prioritizing their faith in Jesus for decades. The problem is, relationships that start in worship services often remain in worship services. What might happen if those relationships extended beyond Sunday morning? What might happen if teens had the opportunity to hear the saints of our congregations share the stories of their faith?

To facilitate this kind of interaction between teens and the saints of my congregation, once a year we visit older members of our church in their homes. During these visits, teens interview the saints and ask them poignant questions about their families, their involvement in church, and their relationships with Christ.

During one such visit, an elderly man pulled out the bulletin from the very first worship service held at our church more than 50 years ago. He shared his memories from that first worship service and then threw down the gauntlet, telling my teens how he's rarely missed a worship service since then because of how important the church—and more importantly, his faith in Jesus—is to him. Through both his words and a bulletin from more than 50 years ago, this man clearly showed my teens it's not only possible, but important, to prioritize faith.

LET TEENS LEAD

Another way to help teens prioritize their faith and their involvement in church is to let them lead, or at least contribute, to our congregations. Encouraging teens to contribute to the community shows their value. It says, "Without you, our community suffers." It transforms them from church consumers to faith producers. In the process, it gives teens ownership of their faith. Once they have that, they cannot help but prioritize it.

To be clear, we must give teens the opportunity to lead more than just their peers. We should allow them to contribute to and even lead our entire congregations. One fantastic way of doing this is to involve teens in worship in ways that utilize their unique gifts. Invite gifted young public speakers to read Scripture or prayers. Ask teen musicians to play with the praise band, sing in the choir, or do a special musical piece. Invite those with a heart for welcoming others to be greeters or ushers.

For several years now, my congregation has been experimenting with this. Our worship is liturgically based, and one of the roles we have is an assisting minister who serves as a cantor, singing various pieces of the liturgy. The assisting minister also prays and helps with Communion. One teen, who spent two years in this role, came from a family for whom worship was not a priority. Yet, when she was asked to serve in this role, worship became a priority for her. Not only that, but worship became a priority for her family as well.

Another young person, one who was far more active in my youth ministry, also served in this role for multiple years. Even though this teen faithfully attended youth group, participated in youth retreats and trips, and was a student leader in my youth ministry, when I asked her what helped her faith grow the most, she consistently pointed to her experience as an assisting minister. That experience made her acutely aware of the words of the liturgy and of God's presence in her life and in the community of faith. It forced her to prioritize her faith, and that, in turn, strengthened her understanding of Jesus.

RAISE THE BAR

In addition to giving teens opportunities to contribute to your greater church community, encourage them to do the same within your youth ministry. Give them opportunities to lead. When you do, don't settle for halfhearted leadership. Instead, raise the bar.

Several years ago, I sat in a meeting with my student leadership team. In the midst of it, one of my student leaders spoke up. With passion she exclaimed, "You need to expect more of us, Jen!"

That experience was a transformative moment for me. It was the day I started expecting more of my leaders. Among other things, it was the day I stopped giving students token leadership roles and began giving them real leadership roles, the kind that are necessary for our youth ministry to flourish.

Now my student leaders are responsible for communication. They give weekly announcements at our gatherings and manage our Twitter account. They're responsible for creating a culture of welcome within our youth ministry. They live out our motto "Be awkward so others don't have to" by stepping outside of their normal friend groups in order to hang out with our more peripheral young people. Beyond that, they help cast vision for our ministry. They even plan and lead events and discussions that fit within that vision.

Why?

Because doing so makes them prioritize not only their church attendance, but also their faith. By being awkward so others don't have to, teens live out Jesus' teaching to "love your neighbor as yourself." In planning and leading a discussion, they dig deeper into Scripture and, in the process, deepen their own faith while simultaneously ministering to their peers.

MODEL IT

Teens come equipped with built-in lie detectors. They smell hypocrisy from a mile away and they want no part of it. As a result, at the same time you help teens learn to prioritize their faith, it's imperative you model what it looks like to prioritize yours. Talk openly and honestly about the importance of Jesus to your faith.

Let teens see you living out your faith in the world around them. Talk about how and when you serve (outside the times you've got teens in tow). Discuss how faith informs your decisions about things including, but not limited to, where you spend your time and money. Admit the times you fail to love others as Christ loves you, but also share the times you experience the joy that comes from encountering Jesus in and through others.

IT'S NOT JUST ABOUT SELF-PERPETUATION

As much as we might like to return to the era when church was at the center of American life, we can't. We can, however, creatively help teens prioritize their faith, even in a world that no longer assumes it's important. Doing so is about much more than a twisted sense of legalism.

It's about what I found in my research: The more important adolescents say Jesus is to their faith, the stronger their Christologies. If that's true, then when we tell our youth, either implicitly or explicitly, that anything and everything is more important than church and their faith in Jesus, we're not doing them any favors.

To be clear, this isn't about the self-perpetuation of our ministries and churches.

It's about wanting teens to be lifelong followers of Jesus.

CHAPTER NOTES

1. Jon Huckins with Rob Yackley, *Thin Places: Six Postures for Creating and Practicing Missional Community* (Kansas City, MO: The House Studio, 2012), 123.

2. Christianity Today International, "Letters to the Editor," *Christianity Today*, September 7, 2012, www.christianitytoday.com/ct/2012/september/letters-to-the-editor.html.

3. Kenda Creasy Dean and Ron Foster, *The Godbearing Life: The Art of Soul Tending for Youth Ministry* (Nashville: Upper Room Books, 1998), 50.

4. Frederick Buechner, *Wishful Thinking: A Theological ABC* (San Francisco: Harper & Row, 1973), 95. http://frederickbuechner.com/content/place-god-calls-you.

5. Kara E. Powell, Brad M. Griffin, and Cheryl A. Crawford, *Sticky Faith, Youth Worker Edition: Practical Ideas to Nurture Long-term Faith in Teenagers* (Grand Rapids, MI: Zondervan/Youth Specialties, 2011), 75.

CHAPTER 8
STRENGTHEN THE CHRISTOLOGY OF PARENTS

I spent my first year in youth ministry entirely frustrated by parents. The congregation I served at that time had a long history of youth worker turnover. As a result, parents stepped in to ensure that regardless of the tenure of a youth worker, the church's youth ministry would continue. These parents thought they knew best.

I, however, disagreed.

To me, it was quite clear that most of these well-intentioned parents had little or no relationship with Jesus. As a result, I limited their involvement in our youth ministry. Convinced they had no real value to their own children's faith formation, I relegated them to administrative and fundraising tasks, certain they should leave the actual ministry to me, the professional.

I know. I was unbelievably arrogant. Not to mention, wrong.

After all, research suggests that parents, not youth workers, are the primary influencers in their children's faith. In fact, according to Kenda Creasy Dean, "the National Study of Youth and Religion's [NSYR] most incontrovertible finding is that parents generally 'get what they are,' in religion as in most things ... which means that we can expect the faith of the young people we love to reflect the faith we show them."[1]

WHAT YOUTH WORKERS THINK INFLUENCES TEENS' UNDERSTANDING OF JESUS

Intrigued, I wanted to investigate this phenomenon for myself, particularly as it relates to what teens believe about Jesus. To do so, on the surveys I asked young people to rank six potential factors—parents, pastors, media, youth workers, friends, and Scripture—according to how much each had influenced their understanding of Jesus. The surveys revealed that the three greatest influencers on adolescents' understanding of Jesus were youth workers, pastors, and parents. (See Figure 11.) Factors that were less influential on adolescents' understanding of Jesus were Scripture, friends, and the media.

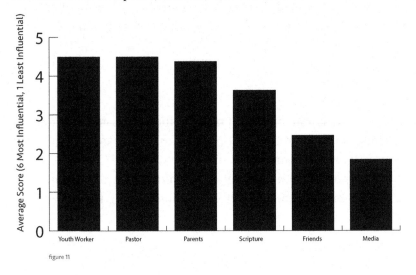

figure 11

Interestingly, youth workers thought friends and media were far more influential on teens' understanding of Jesus than they actually were. When asked who or what was influencing his young people's beliefs about Jesus, one suburban youth worker immediately said, "Their friends are number one." In actuality, his youth group ranked their friends as fifth most influential in their understanding of Jesus, well behind him, their parents, their senior pastor, and Scripture.

After saying that families and parents were the number one influence, a youth worker from the Bible Belt then named peers and the media as the second and third greatest influences on his group's understanding of Jesus. According to him,

146

"They're getting experiences outside the church. There are faith organizations like Young Life. They go with their friends. They go to each other's youth group stuff. Social media also plays into that." While individuals from his group agreed their parents were the most influential factor in their understanding of Jesus, they, too, ranked friends and the media as having the least influence on their understanding of Jesus.

A small-town youth worker was quick to identify parents as the primary influence on her teens' understanding of Jesus. According to her, "What the parents are doing related to their kids' faith has way more influence than me. How faith is treated in the home is going to get a bigger reflection upon their faith." In contrast, however, her teens said parents were the second greatest influence on their faith, not far behind the influence of their senior pastor.

HOW VARIOUS PEOPLE INFLUENCE ADOLESCENTS' UNDERSTANDING OF JESUS

Wanting to learn more about what influences adolescents' understanding of Jesus, I also asked them about any influential factors during focus groups. During the suburban focus group, teens spoke often about the impact their youth director had on their understanding of Jesus. One young person said spending time with him "will change your idea of Christ." Another elaborated, saying, "He helps us see how our faith is related to our lives. That helps us realize who Jesus is."

Other suburban youth pointed to their senior pastor's influence. One said, "I've talked to him about stuff. Whenever I have questions, I can go to him." Others said confirmation leaders and parents also influenced their understanding of Jesus. These responses confirmed the results of the surveys for this population. On it, suburban teens ranked their youth worker, parents, and pastors as the three most dominant influences on their understanding of Jesus.

One thing that was surprising about this suburban congregation was the fact that even though participants' surveys showed parents to be the second largest influence, when asked specifically what they'd had learned from their parents about Jesus, teens froze. The best answer those in this group could come up with was that their parents brought them to church, the place where others then taught them about Jesus.

At the rural focus group, every young person present identified their pastors or parents as the primary influences on their understanding of Jesus. Like their suburban peers, most of them were unable to articulate what these individuals actually taught them about Jesus. In fact, only one had an answer to this question. His was one that quickly reverted to generic God-talk, rather than specific Jesus-talk. I asked: *What did your parents and pastor teach you about Jesus?* He responded, "It's going to be okay. Something's going to go wrong, but God's going to be there. Don't stress too much."

Survey responses from youth at the small-town congregation I visited were much more varied. According to their surveys, the top four influencers on these young people were their pastor, parents, youth worker, and Scripture. Their varied responses were also apparent during my focus group with them. The young people spoke overwhelmingly positively about their pastor's influence and presence. "Pastor's there. He's someone you can go and talk to," said one. Another was careful to say that his pastor's influence was not forced on him. "Pastor's not really pushing you; he's leading you in the right direction."

Young people from this congregation also spoke of the influence their parents had on their understanding of Jesus. As with other congregations, when asked specifically what their parents had taught them about Jesus, otherwise articulate youth were suddenly at a loss for words. Previously specific Jesus-talk became generalized God-talk about a feel-good religion. According to one, "Your parents always told you, you could go to God for help. If I'm ever going through hard times, it's like, 'Say a prayer.' If it happens, it happens. God meant for it to happen." Others said their parents' contribution to their understanding of Jesus was "forcing" them to go to church, although one acknowledged, "If they hadn't done that when I was younger, why would I have started now? It's just the rhythm."

Despite the fact that, according to the survey results, their youth worker was the third most important influencer on their understanding of Jesus, when asked, no youth from this small-town congregation mentioned the youth worker. This was, however, the only congregation whose teens talked about anything besides youth workers, pastors, and parents having influenced their understanding of Jesus. They also mentioned the influence Scripture had on their understanding of Jesus. According to one person, "You always remember the stories, like Zacchaeus. These stories that you hear repeated over and over and over. They really affected me."

These young people were also the only youth from any congregation to acknowledge the two influencers ranked last in the survey results: friends and the media. One went so far as to say, "Peers definitely [influence my understanding of Jesus] more than my parents. I've always gone to church, but we've never really talked about it at home. It's just not a dinner-table conversation. I think you learn different things from your peers. I'm in a Christian group at my school. I like that a lot."

Another young person shared the profound impact the movie *The Passion of Christ* had on his understanding of Jesus.[2] "That [movie] definitely inspired me about what Jesus went through to forgive our sins. That also helped a lot for me to come to church."

Additionally, those from the small-town congregation were the only ones to mention the influence youth group events and trips had on their understanding of Jesus. One girl cited a seventh grade retreat as having been instrumental in teaching her to pray. Several others talked about how much denominational youth gatherings contributed to their identities as Christians.

THE ELEPHANT IN THE ROOM

By now you may have noticed an inconsistency. At the start of this chapter, I told you how parents are the most important spiritual influencers on their child's faith. I then proceeded to tell you how data from both my surveys, as well as my focus groups contradict this, suggesting youth workers and pastors are slightly more influential than parents. So let's talk about the elephant in the room.

Like you, this inconsistency jumped out at me as I studied my results. Since it did, I went back to my data and examined it from a different angle, focusing on what influenced youth with a particular Christology Score. Doing so revealed that the more influential parents are in their teenagers' understanding of Jesus, the better their teenagers' Christologies are.

For young people with a Christology Score of seven, parents were the greatest influencers on their understanding of Jesus. The same was also true of those with a Christology Score of six. In contrast, those with Christology Scores of five and below ranked their parents as the third most significant influence on their understanding of Jesus, following youth workers and pastors.

WHAT PARENTS BELIEVE ABOUT JESUS

Intrigued by this finding, I set out to discover what parents actually believe about Jesus. During my focus groups with them, I asked a series of basic Christology questions.

To begin, I asked parents, *Who is Jesus?* (This was also one of the short-answer questions I asked adolescents on the surveys.) Parents' most frequent response to this question was "Savior."

Since parents typically answered this question very succinctly, I explicitly followed it up with, *What does it mean for Jesus to be our Savior?* The most typical answers I received to this question were, "He paid the ultimate price," or "He was our sacrifice." According to one parent, "Jesus is the ultimate sacrifice. The completion from the Old Testament to the New Testament. There doesn't have to be any sacrifices anymore for the forgiveness of sin."

Parents also frequently told me Jesus "saved us from something." When I pushed them to tell me what that "something" was, common responses included "judgment," "myself," and "sins." In the words of one parent: "[Jesus] paid the ultimate price for me. As a sinner, I hope I'll be spared the judgment that I'm due. He saved me from that judgment. I'm eternally grateful for that." Another parent added that as his Savior, "Jesus was God's most recent, most perfect, and last attempt to reach mankind. What better way to come to earth than as the form of a man?"

After "Savior," the next most common response parents gave to the question of Jesus' identity was "my friend." This response surprised me, though perhaps it shouldn't have since, as we've already discovered, young people also know Jesus is their friend. What they don't know is that Jesus is God.

While parents from various congregations called Jesus both a "representative of God" and the "Son of God," only parents from the congregation with the highest average Christology Score referred to Jesus as God. Those who classified Jesus as the "Son of God" were careful to distinguish him from God. Said one suburban parent, "He was the Son of God. He has a

Father. He's the Son."

Parents also referred to Jesus as an advisor, comforter, "go-to" person, helper, rock, representative of God, and rebel. One parent elaborated on Jesus as a rebel, saying, "He seemed to always be attracted to those people in society who were outcasts, who were not considered part of the mainstream. He associated with people that proper upstanding Jews were not supposed to be associated with."

To learn even more about who parents think Jesus is, I also asked them: *What do you admire about Jesus?* The most common responses to this question were his "acceptance of all people," "forgiveness," and "love." One parent explained:

> I'm a little hesitant to use the word *tolerance*. Jesus was open to everyone. It's not that he overlooked the shortcomings. When he told the woman to go and sin no more, he forgave her but warned her, "Don't do it again." Jesus recognized a civil authority. He was open. He approached us honestly. He didn't have any [misconceptions] of who and what we are. He loved us in spite of us.

Additionally, parents admired Jesus' kindness, peacefulness, and selflessness. By and large, they also respected Jesus as a teacher. One parent said, "He tried to get people to realize and figure things out for themselves." According to parents, the most important things Jesus taught were love, faith, and respect, although it's worth noting that only parents from the two congregations with the highest Christology Scores said Jesus taught faith.

Another question I asked parents was whether or not Jesus sinned, and more parents thought Jesus sinned than thought he was sinless. As with many of the youth I spoke with, one thing

152

that contributed to this belief in parents was a general mistrust of the Bible. According to one:

> Everything we know is from written accounts, written hundreds of years after the fact. Those who are friends with him wrote kindly. I don't know how many texts were not favorable. They weren't going to be included in the Bible.

The parents who thought Jesus was sinless came from the two congregations with the highest average Christology Scores. For them, this belief was central to their faith. According to one parent, "That he didn't sin is the premise our faith is built on." Another added, "If he sinned, we don't have anything to believe in." That this belief was central to them is also reflected in their children's answers to the survey question: *Did Jesus sin?* While only 36 percent of the total number of young people surveyed said Jesus was sinless, 58 percent of the youth from the congregation with the second highest overall Christology Score, and a whopping 83 percent of youth from the congregation with the highest Christology Score affirmed his sinlessness.

After hearing parents discuss their views on whether or not Jesus sinned, I also wanted to hear them articulate their views of the atonement. Few were able to do so. Most who attempted to explain the atonement said Jesus died because it was "God's plan" to "pay the price for our sins" and to "fulfill the prophecies." Others said Jesus died so we wouldn't have to fear death.

Yet another question I asked parents was: *Is Jesus the only way to heaven?* In contrast to their children, more parents agreed than disagreed that Jesus is the only way to heaven. As with their children, however, this was an area in which parents expressed a great deal of uncertainty. One parent put it like this,

"I don't know if it's any of our business if Jesus is the only way to heaven."

Since being in relationship with Jesus is about more than just correct theology, I also asked parents what it means to follow Jesus. Time and time again, they attempted to avoid answering this question by repeating it back to me, saying it meant to "follow Jesus' example." I'd then respond, *What does following that example entail?* At that point, more often than not, parents would say, "Love others."

Aside from love, parents also believe following Jesus entails practicing forgiveness and a laundry list of "right behaviors," including consideration for others, gentleness, humility, kindness, loyalty, niceness, selflessness, and a willingness to share.

It's worth noting that while several of these are fruits of the Spirit, based on how parents described them to me during our time together, others (like loyalty, niceness, and a willingness to share) are not. According to them, being nice means smiling at everyone and keeping the peace, even if it means avoiding hard truths and realities; being loyal means not gossiping about friends; and being willing to share means teens will allow their friends equal playing time on their latest video game.

Are some of these attributes good? Absolutely. But are they what our Christian faith compels us to do? Not quite. Our Christian faith compels us to be kind—even to those who are our enemies; to be loyal, to the point of sacrificially loving someone, even if it means giving up our life for theirs; and to share our goods and resources so that no one is in need (Acts 2:45). Yet, that's not what parents told me these values meant. To them, these values appear more reflective of American culture than Scripture. Is it any wonder then, that American adolescents think Jesus taught the same thing our Founding

Fathers did?

As a church worker, my hope is certainly that Jesus makes a difference in the daily lives of parents and their children alike. To this end, I asked parents: *What difference does Jesus make in your life?* The most common responses to this question were "Jesus gives me an example to follow," "Jesus is the foundation of everything I do," and "He teaches me to appreciate things." Once again, parents from the two congregations with the highest Christology Scores had a much easier time discussing the difference Jesus made in their lives than parents from the two congregations with the weakest Christology Scores.

Parents from the congregations with the strongest Christology Scores talked about how their faith in Jesus influenced their identities, gave them hope and purpose, and energized them. They also talked about practical ways Jesus impacted their daily lives. One said, "There are three differences Jesus makes in my life—the interactions I have with people, how I spend my time, and how my wife and I budget."

I also asked parents what difference they hoped Jesus would make in the lives of their teens. Some parents were adamant about their desire for their children to take ownership of their faith. One mom explained, "She's got to have her own faith. Mine can only carry her so far." According to her, and others like her, the key to making this happen is teaching teens to "vocalize and defend their faith."

Other parents expressed hope that Jesus would give their children identity, purpose, direction, and a sense of vocation. According to one, "I hope that Jesus gives them purpose or direction for their life and where they're headed and service for others—no matter what job they're involved in. I hope that Jesus will be a big part of that and their relationships with people going forward."

Other parents spoke passionately about the companionship they hoped Jesus would provide their children with, constantly giving them someone to "fall back on." Still others expressed a view of Jesus very much in line with Moralistic Therapeutic Deism, likening Jesus to a safety device used to protect their children. One parent even went so far as to say, "I hope my son will believe Jesus is there to help him."

By far, most parents answered this question in terms of morality, suggesting the impact they expect Jesus to have on their children is largely behavioral. To this end, parents expressed their hope that a relationship with Jesus would produce good character in their children, along with things like respect. One even went so far as to say he hoped a relationship with Jesus would solve the dress code issues he was currently having with his child.

PARENT MINISTRY IS YOUTH MINISTRY

Given the influence parents have on their children's faith, it can be discouraging to see how poor some of their Christologies actually are. Even so, throughout the various focus groups I conducted, I was deeply encouraged by parents' desires to improve their own understanding of Jesus and help their children do the same. According to one, "I'm realizing how [possible it is] to go to church every Sunday without saying anything about Jesus outside of church. I'm trying not to make the same mistakes my parents made." Knowing parents care deeply about their children's faith, the question then becomes, how can we help parents strengthen their own Christologies so that they, in turn, can help strengthen their children's beliefs about Jesus?

This starts by recognizing that parent ministry is youth ministry. Ministering to parents is not just a nice thing for us to do; it's a critical part of our ministry to teens. As such, make time for it. Value it. Prioritize it. Then teach and challenge your colleagues to do the same. Parent ministry is not just your job. It's also the job of the senior pastor, family pastor, and musicians. So work collaboratively to invest in parents.

Ensure that conversations about Jesus aren't just limited to one component of your church's ministry, but that they're happening in every part of your congregation. For example, do a sermon series on Jesus' character during weekly worship, but do so without turning Jesus into another moralistic teacher. As part of this, stop speculating about what Jesus might do and instead teach what Jesus did. If your congregation has an education hour, use that time to hold an adult Sunday school class on the foundations of faith. In it, teach the basics of Jesus' life, teachings, death, and resurrection so parents strengthen their Christologies right alongside their children.

INVOLVE PARENTS

Use your words and actions to remind parents they are the most important spiritual influencers in their children's lives. Don't minimize or shut them out, even when they frustrate or irritate you. Create opportunities for them to be involved in their children's faith formation. For example, during our students' senior year of high school, we hold an event for them and their parents. During this event, parents and their kids dream together about their futures, as individuals and as families. They're then given questions to discuss with one another about their hopes and dreams for the future, including their future faith journeys. In this safe environment, parents have the opportunity to speak words about their children's faith that, given the hustle and bustle of life, might otherwise go unspoken.

Another easy way to do this is to host a parents' night during your regular youth group meeting time. Encourage young people to bring their parents to youth group as their guests. Rather than give a sermon, give your youth a passage from one of the Gospels. Ask them to read it together with their parents. Then provide parents with questions to help them dig deeper into the passage and to learn about Jesus together.

For an even easier way of involving parents, each time you meet, email them a two- to three-sentence description of what you're teaching, along with how it relates to Jesus. Then give them three to five questions to spark a conversation with their children. Challenge them to find time during the week, even when they're in the car going to and fro, to discuss those questions with their children.

Outside of weekly events, find ways to include parents in your key ministry events throughout the year. Some of the best ways to do this don't necessarily require parents to be physically present. For example, invite them to write out prayers for their children that you'll then distribute during a mission trip, or find ways to creatively involve them in your retreats.

During a recent high school retreat, I involved parents in a very passive way. The theme of this retreat was seeing and hearing God. Prior to it, I distributed disposable cameras to those going on the retreat and asked them to take one photo during each hour of their day. I then developed those photos and had each person make a collage during the retreat. Most of my group's collages featured pictures of their families, including their parents. We then asked teens to consider where—in the course of the day they'd photographed—they'd seen and heard God (something that was much easier for them to identify in hindsight). Parents became an integral part of the retreat weekend simply because they were featured prominently in the collages.

Another way of involving parents in retreats is to invite them to write a letter to their children related to the weekend's theme. I invited parents to do this for our seeing and hearing

God retreat. Specifically, I asked parents to name the gifts God had given their teenagers, along with how they'd seen Jesus at work in their teens' lives. At the emotional high point of the weekend, the adult leaders then distributed these letters to teens. In so doing, we linked teens to parents—and to their parents' faith—rather than to ours. At the same time, since parents had also put thought into reflecting on our topic, we set parents up to have conversations with their kids after the retreat. As one mom told me, "This was a very easy and wonderful assignment!"

As you search for creative ways to involve parents, look outside the walls of your youth room. Hold a storytelling event for families in your congregation. At this event, bring people together over a meal. Then hand out large sheets of butcher paper to each person present, young and old alike. Direct people to draw their "faithline"—a timeline of the key events in their journeys of faith including, but not limited to, significant experiences, trips, people, and moments when they encountered Christ. After giving people time to create their faithlines, give families time to share theirs with one another. Don't assume family members already know each other's faith stories. Most don't, even though the College Transition Project (*Sticky Faith, Youth Worker Edition*) showed us that parents sharing about their own faith is vital to the process of a child growing into his or her own.[3]

SEIZE THE TIME YOU ALREADY HAVE

Unfortunately, the reality is that in most churches, our response to a felt need is programmatic. If parents have weak Christologies, we immediately wonder what programs we can implement to strengthen them. To some degree, the solutions I've already suggested are, in fact, programmatic. Yet, during the focus groups I held with parents, one thing I heard again and again was, "We don't want another program." Parents are busy with work, extracurricular activities, chauffeuring their kids, and other commitments. They don't want to do or go to anything else.

Knowing this, figure out how to strengthen parents' Christologies without adding more programs. To begin, seize the time you already have with parents. During parent meetings, include a short testimony from someone about how he or she has encountered Christ in his or her life. Alternatively, do a short teaching relevant to the topic at hand.

During a logistics and safe-child policy meeting, read Jesus' commands in Luke 10:26-28, " 'Love the Lord your God with all your heart and with all your soul and with all your strength and with all your mind'; and, 'Love your neighbor as yourself.'" As you share the vision for your youth ministry, discuss how each different facet of your ministry helps teens love the Lord with all their hearts, souls, strength, and minds. As you delve into the safe-child policy, explain how protecting children and teens is an act of love; how setting up a safe sanctuary for teens and leaders enables them to more fully "love their neighbors as themselves."

Likewise, during a meeting about your summer mission trip, take time to explore the parable of the sheep and the goats that Jesus tells in Matthew 25:31-46. Wrestle with how your team will live out that passage during the upcoming trip.
In the same way, whenever you meet one-on-one with parents, take time to talk together about Jesus. Courageously ask parents about their walks with Christ. Invite them to share the ways in which Jesus is influencing their daily lives. Give them the space to confess their struggles. Ask how you can pray for and support not just the faith of the child with whom you work most directly, but their faith as well. In addition to encouraging parents in their faith journeys, such conversations will also strengthen your relationships with parents.

As part of the research I did for my christological foundations class project, I interviewed parents in my congregation to better understand their beliefs about Jesus. During one such visit, I sat with the mom of one the young people in my youth ministry. I asked her questions about Jesus, including: *What Jesus story do you relate to the most?*

She then recounted how much she related to the story of Jesus weeping outside Lazarus' tomb. When I asked her why, she explained how during a recent struggle that her child had faced, she constantly imagined Jesus there, weeping with her child. She said that image carried her through that time. As this mom shared this story with me, tears filled her eyes. Before long, tears filled mine as well. What began as a simple interview turned into one of the most profound moments of my career.

HELP THEM LET GO

During adolescence, teens undergo individuation. As Mark Oestreicher states in his book *Youth Ministry 3.0*: "This process is primarily (though not exclusively) the issue of separating from one's family."[4] As part of it, teens quite naturally question their faith in Jesus, as well as the beliefs with which they've been raised.

As youth workers, one gift we can give to parents is to help normalize this experience. Reach out to them and explain that not only is this an expected part of adolescence, but it's a necessary part of taking ownership of one's faith. Reassure parents that even during those times when teens may appear to have abandoned Jesus, Jesus hasn't abandoned them.

RESOURCE PARENTS

Most youth workers understand that part of our calling is to offer resources to parents, providing basic counseling and information about a variety of topics including social media, self-harm, and school. Far fewer of us ever think to provide parents with resources about Jesus. So stock your shelves with books about Jesus and invite parents to check them out. Having spent the better part of the last two years immersing myself in this subject, ones I'd recommend—not necessarily for their theology, but rather for their conversation-sparking potential—include:

- *Who Is Jesus?* by Carl Braaten (Eerdmans, 2011)
- *Searching for God Knows What* by Donald Miller (Thomas Nelson, 2004)
- *The Meaning of Jesus: Two Visions* by Marcus Borg and N. T. Wright (HarperOne, 1999)
- *Relearning Jesus* by Matthew Paul Turner (David C. Cook, 2009)
- *Unholy Night* by Seth Grahame-Smith (Hachette, 2010)
- *My Imaginary Jesus: The Spiritual Adventures of One Man Searching for the Real God* by Matt Mikalatos (Tyndale, 2012)
- *The Challenge of Jesus: Rediscovering Who Jesus Was and Is* by N. T. Wright (InterVarsity, 1999)

Consider inviting parents to discuss these books with you after they finish reading them—whether in person or via phone or email. Then challenge them to discuss them with their teens.

IF I HAD TO DO IT OVER AGAIN

If I could go back to my first year in ministry, there's so much I'd do differently. Having learned that "parents generally 'get what they are' in religion"[5] and that the more influential parents are in their children's understanding of Jesus, the better teens' Christologies are, instead of relegating parents to the background, now I'd give them a prominent place in my ministry. I'd do so regardless of how much they know about Jesus.

Rather than judging parents for their beliefs, I'd find out what they believe about Jesus and then, using the strategies I've outlined in this chapter, I'd build upon or, if necessary, even challenge that understanding.

Of course the truth is, I can't go back. And to be honest, that pains me. I know I did the teens in my first congregation a disservice by undervaluing their parents. After all, the Christologies of teens are intricately connected to the Christologies of their parents.

However, since I know that now, I won't make the same mistake again. Today, you'll find me investing in parents and, in particular, their Christologies.

I hope you'll join me.

Doing so will greatly influence our teenagers' understanding of Jesus, perhaps far more than anything else we'll ever do.

CHAPTER NOTES

1. Kenda Creasy Dean, *Almost Christian: What the Faith of our Teenagers Is Telling the American Church* (New York: Oxford University Press, 2010), 39.

2. Jim Caviezel, Monica Bellucci, et al. *The Passion of the Christ* (Beverly Hills, CA: 20th Century Fox, 2004).

3. Kara E. Powell, Brad M. Griffin, and Cheryl A. Crawford, *Sticky Faith, Youth Worker Edition: Practical Ideas to Nurture Long-term Faith in Teenagers* (Grand Rapids, MI: Zondervan/Youth Specialties, 2011), 118.

4. Mark Oestreicher, *Youth Ministry 3.0: A Manifesto of Where We've Been, Where We Are, and Where We Need to Go* (Grand Rapids, MI: Zondervan/Youth Specialties, 2008), 40.

5. Dean, *Almost Christian,* 39.

CHAPTER 9

SHARE YOUR FAITH

I remember how during a job interview at a church, I excitedly told the pastor about an event that my previous church had held for the refugee community. This event was largely relational in focus and designed to give the youth an opportunity to get to know people from different cultures. During it, we played games and hosted a barbecue. At the end of the day, we distributed backpacks filled with school supplies to the children.

After hearing this, the pastor asked, "Did you evangelize during that event?"

To be honest, I thought I detected a hint of worry in her voice as she asked her question.

Nevertheless, I answered truthfully, explaining that some but not all of the refugees who attended this event were Christians. I told the pastor that while we didn't do a formal presentation of the gospel, as we'd prepared for the event, we discussed how sometimes our actions can provide us with opportunities to share our faith with others. In the hope that this might happen, we prepared teens to share their faith one-on-one with people if the opportunity arose. In doing so, I'd hoped to teach them to live out 1 Peter 3:15, "Always be prepared to give an answer to everyone who asks you to give the reason for the hope that you have. But do this with gentleness and respect."

I felt good about my response to this interview question until the pastor said, "Well, in our tradition, we respect the faith of others. We don't evangelize."

Despite being a bit taken aback by the strength of this pastor's conviction not to witness to others, in truth, I let out a deep sigh of relief. The fact that this church didn't evangelize didn't bother me.

At the time, I didn't evangelize either.

Years before, I'd been sitting in a Purpose Driven Youth Ministry Conference listening to youth ministry guru Doug Fields explain the five purposes of youth ministry: worship, discipleship, evangelism, ministry, and fellowship. After doing so, Doug asked, "Which of these purposes are you most passionate about? Which do you bleed?"

I remember thinking, *I'm not sure which one I'm most passionate about, but I can certainly tell you which one I'm least passionate about: evangelism.*

Having grown up in the Methodist tradition, I'd never even heard of evangelism until I got to college. And I initially associated evangelism exclusively with the street preacher who stood on the quad yelling that fornicators were damned for hell. My peers universally thought this preacher was crazy. I interpreted their reaction to mean this type of evangelism was counterproductive.

Unfortunately, my campus pastor bled evangelism. Rather than let this street preacher shape our understanding of evangelism, he countered it with his own. At one of our worship services, he showed a clip from the movie *Titanic.* The clip takes place after the boat sinks, when the few survivors are left clinging to floating chunks of ice, hoping a boat will come and rescue them. Our pastor said those people represented those without Jesus. According to him, non-Christians are clinging to a rapidly disappearing iceberg, waiting for someone—namely us—to rescue them with the message of Jesus.

Clearly, the message had an impact on me. Fifteen years later, I still vividly remember it.

Even so, at the time I sat there thinking, *He's not talking about me. He can't expect me to rescue all those drowning people. I'm an introvert. God didn't bless me with the gift of evangelism.*

Right or wrong, that way of thinking shaped my first decade in youth ministry. Since I didn't feel passionate about evangelism, I seldom emphasized it with my youth.

I regret that now.

After all, more than just being one of the five purposes of youth ministry, my research shows a relationship between teens' willingness to talk about their faith with others and the strength of their Christologies.

HOW OFTEN DO TEENS TALK ABOUT JESUS?

Clearly, it wasn't my own passion for evangelism that led me to explore the relationship between it and Christologies. Instead, it was Kenda Creasy Dean's conclusion in *Almost Christian* that "conversational Christianity requires Jesus-talk, not just God-talk."[1] Intrigued by this conclusion, on the surveys I asked high school students to rank how frequently they talked specifically about Jesus (not just God) in their youth ministries, with their friends, and with their families. To do so, they used this scale:

every time we meet OR daily / weekly / monthly / yearly / never

Responses were then assigned a number and averaged within each category. A Jesus-talk score of five meant adolescents talked about Jesus all the time, whereas a Jesus-talk score of one meant they never spoke of him.

Not surprisingly, young people talked about Jesus the most with their youth ministries, which earned a score of 4.5, meaning most youth ministries talked about Jesus at least weekly, if not every time they met. Talking about Jesus with young people's families earned an average score of 3.2, which means most families talked about Jesus on a monthly basis. Youth confessed to talking about Jesus the least with their friends, which earned an average score of 2.4. In other words, adolescents talked about Jesus with their friends only sporadically, on somewhere between a monthly and yearly basis.

Though somewhat disappointing to me, this result was not surprising. After all, in both youth ministries and families, adolescents likely retain little control over what they talk about. If youth workers or parents want to talk about Jesus, young people will be forced to do so. In contrast, in their relationships with friends, teens choose what they discuss. It seems reasonable, then, that in that kind of relationship teens will only discuss Jesus if he's important to them.

THE RELATIONSHIP BETWEEN EVANGELISM AND CHRISTOLOGY

Having realized this, I began to wonder if there was a relationship between the strength of teens' Christologies and their willingness to talk about Jesus with their friends. To find out, I compared teens' Christology Scores with their Jesus-talk scores. (See Figure 12.) This showed that regardless of the strength of their Christologies, adolescents are talking about Jesus in their youth ministries.

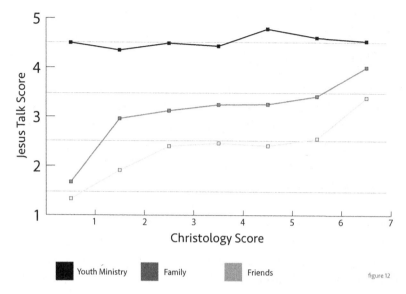

Youth Ministry   Family   Friends

My comparison between Christology and Jesus-talk scores also showed that the higher teens' Christology Scores were, the more they talked about Jesus with both their family and friends. Consider, for a moment, how frequently teens talk about Jesus with their friends. Youth with the highest Christology Score had an average Jesus-talk score of 3.4 with their friends, which means they talked about Jesus somewhere between once a week and once a month. This is nearly a full point (0.83) higher than those with the next highest Christology Score. Their average Jesus-talk is 2.6, meaning they talked about Jesus with their friends somewhere between once a month and once a year.

To be clear, from my research I cannot tell you what impacts what. Do young people with strong Christologies naturally talk about Jesus more often with their friends than teens with weaker Christologies do? Or does talking about Jesus with their friends actually strengthen teens' Christologies?

Regardless of which direction this relationship flows, what's clear from my research is that it doesn't just matter *what* we say about Jesus; it also matters *who* we talk with about him. This, of course, has important implications for ministry.

REDEFINE EVANGELISM

Since the *who* and the *what* of evangelism are equally important, then in addition to addressing the specific aspects of Christology that we've discussed thus far in this book, we've also got to intentionally use our youth ministries to equip teens to share their faith with their friends. This begins with reframing evangelism.

So often, we in the church talk about evangelism as a command. We point to Matthew 28:19-20 and say, "Look, Jesus commanded us to evangelize. He said, 'Therefore go and make disciples ... baptizing them in the name of the Father and of the Son and of the Holy Spirit, and teaching them to obey everything that I have commanded you.' "

The problem with this is twofold. In *Evangelism Remixed*, Dave Rahn and Terry Linhart explain that making evangelism a command makes it just one more thing to do that, in their words, "only contributes to the burdensome pile-on that so many of us experience in ministry."[2] More problematic still, when this happens, evangelism becomes our job rather than the work of the Holy Spirit.

Instead of viewing evangelism as a command, let's view it as the natural overflow of a life centered on Jesus. Consider Jesus' words: "For the mouth speaks what the heart is full of" (Matthew 12:34b).

One of the things I'm passionate about is refugee ministry, so it's natural for me to find ways—sometimes unexpected ways—to bring it up in conversation. Although I'm introverted, once I start talking about refugee ministry, it's hard for me to stop. I can talk excitedly about it for hours on end. Thus, during the decade I've spent doing this type of ministry, on more than one occasion people have remarked, "Is there any conversation you *can't* turn toward refugees?"

So it is with Jesus. When we're passionate about our relationship with him, it's natural for us to talk excitedly about him—not just in the forums where it's expected, like at church, but also with our friends and family members. When that happens, evangelism stops being the scary thing reserved only for one specific personality type, and it becomes something we cannot help but do. In short, it becomes what Rahn and Linhart call part of "the faithfulness mix."[3]

GO OLD SCHOOL

Once you've redefined evangelism, ground teens in Christ. For young people to be able to share their faith with others, they must first know Jesus. Work through the strategies in this book to strengthen teens' beliefs about Jesus.

As you do, incorporate regular opportunities for teens to share their testimonies—the stories of what Jesus is doing in their lives—within your youth ministry. Inviting teens to share their faith within your youth ministry enables them to practice doing so in a safe environment where, rather than being perceived as weird, talking about Jesus is expected.

Do this both informally and formally. Informally, include testimony-focused questions in regular discussions. For example, at the end of every small group gathering, ask teens to answer the question: *Where did you encounter Jesus this week?* Doing so will challenge them to find the intersection of their stories and God's story.

More formally, model how to give a testimony to young people by sharing your own and inviting other adult leaders to do the same. In so far as they are useful, teach teens formulas to help them prepare to share their faith stories. For example, in his youth ministry classic *Purpose-Driven Youth Ministry*, Doug Fields offers a formula based on the example of Paul before Agrippa in Acts 26:1-23. According to this formula, a testimony consists of sharing your attitudes and actions before you became a Christian, the circumstances surrounding your conversion, and the changes in your attitudes and actions since your conversion.[4]

Another formula you can use to help teens prepare their testimonies is the seven-word faith story. In this formula, limit teens to only seven words to describe their faith in Jesus. While some teens will find this impossibly hard, it will free others, especially introverts, from believing that testimonies must always be lengthy. You'll also be amazed at the creativity and depth teens are able to communicate in only seven words.

Yet another way of teaching teens to share their faith stories is to use a picture of a flower, like a daisy, where all the petals are connected to a central point. Give everyone in your group a physical, black-and-white drawing of such a flower. In the center of their flowers, ask them to write Jesus—the person who stands at the center of their faith. Then ask them to add to each of the flower petals the significant people, events, and experiences that have influenced their faith in Jesus. Once everyone has filled in their flowers, they can then use them to share their faith stories. Rather than speaking linearly about their faith journeys, teach them to talk about them by relating each part back to Jesus.

Regardless of how teens prepare their faith stories, once they've done so, be intentional about inviting them to share those stories in your youth ministry. There is, after all, power in hearing how Jesus is at work in the lives of others. When teens hear about the difference Jesus has made in their friends' lives, they begin to believe he can make a difference in theirs as well.

That said, as you listen to teens share their testimonies, affirm them. When necessary, challenge them as well. In particular, be on the lookout for faith stories that exclude Jesus. Whenever you hear one, directly ask that young person about the role Jesus plays in his or her faith. Then invite the teen to find a way to include that in the testimony and once again share it with the group.

SHARE TESTIMONIES IN CHURCH

To further equip teens to talk about Jesus with their friends, invite them to take baby steps outside of their comfort zones by first sharing their testimonies—maybe the same one they've already practiced—with your larger community of faith. Since the people in your faith community are used to hearing about Jesus, talking about him won't be perceived as weird. At the same time, since teens in your congregation probably aren't used to talking about their faith with those outside of your youth ministry, this will give them new people to practice on. This, in turn, will help teens grow more comfortable talking about Jesus with others.

One way my congregation does this is by giving high school seniors the opportunity to preach during worship. Prior to the worship service, we work with them to help prepare their sermons, which are essentially their faith stories juxtaposed with Gospel passages chosen for the day. Similar to asking teens where they encountered Jesus that week, this process helps them find the intersection between their stories and God's story. Since this is a sermon, we always invite teens to give the congregation a challenge of some sort. This forces them to begin thinking about where their story and God's story intersect with the stories of others.

BATHE THE PROCESS IN PRAYER

As you cultivate an environment in which teens are increasingly comfortable talking about Jesus, bathe the process in prayer. Returning to the work of youth ministry experts Rahn and Linhart in *Evangelism Remixed*:

> Group prayer is a cornerstone activity for
> evangelistically effective teens and youth groups ...
> when groups reported that they prayed together for
> lost friends on a weekly basis, God moved through
> them to help their peers believe in Jesus in pretty
> remarkable ways.[5]

Given this, teach teens to pray not just for one another, but also for those outside the church. Invite them to pray not just for their "lost friends" to know Christ, but for the steps in between. Challenge teens to pray for opportunities to talk about not just church or their spirituality with their friends, but specifically about Jesus.

As a result of the findings from my research, I've recently begun experimenting with this in my own student leadership team. At the end of last summer, I gave my leadership team a challenge. I told them that since I've seen the powerful ways God has moved through our ministry, I wanted others to experience that as well. With that in mind, I laid out the goal of doubling the size of our youth ministry.

Now, let me tell you right off the bat that we failed colossally to reach this goal. That said, it was still a goal worth setting. In trying to reach it, our team intentionally and consistently prayed for opportunities to talk about Jesus with people. Nine months later, we're still reaping the fruit of this, both in the youth who have come to our ministry as a result of this intentionality, as well as in my student leaders.

Although one of my student leaders had previously refused to talk with her friends about anything related to her faith, after I issued this challenge, she decided to go for it. Slowly but surely, she began talking about Jesus with her friends. And in the process, she invited them to our youth ministry not because we were hosting a "Bring a Friend Sunday," but because it was a natural overflow of her passion for Jesus and our youth ministry. The more this girl talked with her friends about Jesus, the more natural it became to invite them to a safe place where they, too, could talk about Jesus. She did so confidently knowing that when she invited her friends to attend, we would, in fact, be talking about Jesus.

Why?

Because her own experience taught her that we talk about Jesus every time we meet.

LET YOUTH LEAD

Besides knowing we'd talk about Jesus, another reason this girl initially brought her friends to our youth ministry was because of her leadership responsibilities in it. Early on during the school year, this young person led one of our discussions. She planned, wrote, edited, and facilitated it.

For years, I've been a proponent of student-led discussions because my own experience has taught me that I learn most when I'm teaching someone else. Knowing this, I've long since believed that youth learn best and grow in their faith the most when they teach or lead discussions.

What I've seen throughout this year has only added to my belief that such opportunities are incredibly important to the faith formation and specifically to the christological formation of teens. Student-led discussions give teens the space and motivation to talk with their peers about faith and, more importantly, Jesus.

PROCESS AND DEBRIEF EVANGELISM

Throughout my years in youth ministry, I've become a fan of team-building. An often-repeated mantra in team-building is "Anything worth doing is worth processing." In recent years, our youth ministry world has also adopted this approach in regard to short-term missions. This suggests, as Kara Powell and Brad Griffin do in *Deep Justice Journeys*, that effective justice ministries require work before, during, and after justice experiences, and that a critical component of the work done afterward is processing and debriefing.[6] If processing and debriefing team-builders and justice work increases the long-term effectiveness of these endeavors, why would we not assume the same is also true with evangelism?

When it goes well, talking with others about Jesus can be life-giving and, in many ways, exhilarating. But sometimes talking with others about Jesus is hard. Sometimes attempts to talk about him are, quite simply, rejected. In either case, teens need the opportunity to process their experiences and share what they did and why; how it felt to put themselves—and Jesus—out there; what they learned in the process; and how they encountered Jesus as they shared him with others.

As teens share, they need to hear about our own experiences with evangelism. Specifically, they need to hear about the times when our attempts to talk with someone about Jesus ended horribly. This will help teens know and believe they're not alone. To that end, as teens process their experiences with us, encourage them. Let them know you're proud of them for courageously talking about Jesus with others, regardless of how well or poorly he's received.

Over the last nine months, I've done a lot of this processing with the student leader I mentioned earlier. We've celebrated those times when the conversations with her friends have gone well, and we've wrestled with what happened when they've gone poorly. Recently, I received a student leadership application from this same individual. On it, she wrote, "This year I have been so excited about my faith because of the way it's been impacting my relationship with my friends."

In a follow-up conversation with her, she proceeded to elaborate on what she's learned about Jesus through this evangelism process. She talked about immersing herself in the Gospels in order to learn more about Jesus so she could feel confident enough to talk to her friends about him. Her face aglow, she then recounted what her friends have learned about Jesus from her. Perhaps most significantly, she shared how her relationship with them has grown because Jesus is now a central part of it.

IT'S MORE THAN A CHURCH-GROWTH STRATEGY

If you'd told me a decade ago that I'd be writing about evangelism, I'd have called you crazy. In those days, I left evangelism to the street preachers and the extroverts.

Nowadays, I can't imagine *not* equipping teens to talk about Jesus with others. Doing so is more than a church-growth strategy. It's a critical part of discipleship and, in particular, strengthening the Christology of teens.

CHAPTER NOTES

1. Kenda Creasy Dean, *Almost Christian: What the Faith of Our Teenagers Is Telling the American Church* (New York: Oxford University Press, 2010), 139.

2. Dave Rahn and Terry Linhart, *Evangelism Remixed: Empowering Students for Courageous and Contagious Faith* (Grand Rapids, MI: Zondervan/Youth Specialties, 2009), 15.

3. Ibid., 26.

4. Doug Fields, *Purpose-Driven Youth Ministry: 9 Essential Foundations for Healthy Growth* (Grand Rapids, MI. Zondervan/Youth Specialties, 1998), 134.

5. Rahn and Linhart, *Evangelism Remixed*, 26.

6. Kara Powell and Brad Griffin, *Deep Justice Journeys: 50 Activities to Move from Mission Trips to Missional Living* (Grand Rapids, MI: Zondervan/Youth Specialties, 2009), 9.

SECTION 3

WHAT'S THE POINT?

CHAPTER 10

THE DIFFERENCE JESUS MAKES

As a young child, the difference Jesus made in my life was that I went to church.

In high school, the difference Jesus made in my life was that to follow his example, I served the "least of these"—not necessarily in my daily life, but at least during weeklong summer mission trips.

In college, Jesus limited what I could do. Believing in him meant I couldn't drink alcohol or have sex.

As an adult, Jesus makes a huge difference in my life, not by limiting me, but by giving me true freedom. Beyond that, Jesus makes a difference in my life in numerous other ways. He influences my decisions daily. My faith in him gives me a lens through which I view the world. He influences my interactions with others. His love for me both challenges and enables me to love others. Perhaps most importantly, he gives me an identity—one that establishes my worth not based on what I do, but on whose I am.

WHAT IT MEANS TO FOLLOW JESUS

As a youth worker, I hope Jesus makes a profound difference in the lives of young people. To find out if he does, I included this in my research. Of course, for Jesus to make a difference in our lives, we have to follow him. Knowing this, during my focus groups I asked participants: *What does it mean to follow Jesus?*

Their answers to this question fell into two categories: beliefs and actions.

In terms of beliefs, young people indicated that to follow Jesus, you must believe in him, accept him, have Jesus in your heart, know that he's there, and trust he loves you. Unfortunately, because of adolescents' inability to elaborate on or explain these popular Christian phrases, I suspect they reveal more about the culture in which teenagers are raised than they do about what teens actually believe about Jesus.

More telling, perhaps, is what teens said people had to do in order to follow Jesus. According to them, first and foremost, to follow Jesus means to "be like Jesus." In other words, teens believe, as one put it: "You got to let him be your example."

According to teens, following Jesus' example means loving others. In particular, it means helping and caring for others. According to one teen, "You have to let his spirit and passion for justice and equality for religion fill you and affect your actions."

Following Jesus also means, according to those I asked, not judging others. It means worshiping. Specifically, young people discussed the importance of prayer and forgiveness. Teens also talked frequently about how following Jesus means "walking with him." When asked to further explain this, teens described how important it is to keep Jesus a part of your life by "maintaining a good connection" with him.

For some youth, maintaining a good connection with Jesus includes involving him in decision-making. One young person said, "Before you make a decision, bad or good, you think, *Is this what Jesus would want me to do?*" Others equated involving Jesus in their decisions by asking: *What would Jesus do?*

Still others said following Jesus means going to church. In the words of one: "I go to church. That's what determines a follower of Jesus." Others disputed this, suggesting that following Jesus means being "all in." According to one, "A lot of people think they can compartmentalize God: 'Sunday and Wednesday, I'm going to be a Christian.' That's not following Jesus. You can't walk a middle ground."

JESUS DOESN'T MAKE A DIFFERENCE

Once again, I was interested in what it means to teens to follow Jesus because ultimately, I wanted to know how, if at all, Jesus makes a difference in the lives of young people. To begin determining this, on the surveys I asked adolescents whether they agreed or disagreed with the statement: *My faith in Jesus helps me find meaning and purpose in life.* The overwhelming majority (84 percent) agreed with this statement.

To learn more about how Jesus helps adolescents find meaning and purpose in their lives, I asked young people in my focus groups to answer this question: *What, if any, difference does Jesus make in your everyday life?*

One of every ten (or 10 percent) of those present in all focus groups said, "He doesn't." One who admitted this confessed, "I find myself struggling to incorporate God in my everyday life." Another added, "It's hard to hear him in my life and interpret what he's trying to say."

For others, Jesus failed to make a difference in their lives because they found it easier to ignore him than to allow him to influence their daily lives. For them, following Jesus required too much, including sacrificing their futures. One individual saw a clear choice between excelling in school and following Jesus. According to her, "It's such a hard decision between possibly jeopardizing my future and following Jesus."

Other young people explained Jesus didn't make a difference in their lives because they'd relegated him to the background.

According to one, "I'm going to be honest and say Jesus rarely comes up in my life. I don't walk through the hall and think, *What would Jesus be doing right now?* He comes into my life when I really need him." Another expressed a similar sentiment, saying, "God is definitely in the background of my life a good majority of the time."

Both sentiments correspond to findings from the National Study of Youth and Religion, which, as we learned in the introduction, says teens adhere to Moralistic Therapeutic Deism. One of the central tenets of this belief system is that "God does not need to be particularly involved in one's life except when God is needed to resolve a problem."[1]

The second wave of this study, outlined by Christian Smith and Patricia Snell in *Souls in Transition*, found that for most emerging adults, religion is nothing more than a "lifestyle accessory," something that's relegated to the "background."[2] According to Smith, "Religion is simply not important or relevant enough to everyday life to warrant any real discussion."[3] When push comes to shove, religious ideas are, for most emerging adults, mere "abstract agreements that have been mentally checked off and filed away" rather than something people build their lives around.[4]

JESUS PROVIDES

The presence of Moralistic Therapeutic Deism was also clearly evident in adolescents who said Jesus makes a difference in their lives by providing for them, in particular, in times of need. In the words of one teen, "I tend to look for God just when I'm in trouble or need." Similarly, others said Jesus makes a difference in their lives simply by being present, by knowing there's always someone to talk to. According to others, Jesus provides them with a kind of cosmic protection, constantly watching over their lives. Some young people also said Jesus gives them guidance for "deciding how you would handle certain situations and do certain things."

Still others said Jesus provides them with a new perspective. Most commonly, this perspective was that "everything happens for a reason." Similarly, youth said Jesus makes a difference in their lives because of his plans for them. One teen said, "Every day if something happens, I think it was God's plan for me."

Mind you, throughout Scripture God does, in fact, provide. However, in contrast to the cosmic genie mentality many youth have, the God of the Bible provides for all people, not just his followers. As Matthew 5:45 says, "He causes his sun to rise on the evil and the good, and sends rain on the righteous and the unrighteous."

Interestingly, those who seemed to have the most biblical understanding of God's provision were from the rural congregation—the one with the lowest average Christology Score. According to one youth:

> Jesus makes all the difference. We live on a farm. You gotta believe or we wouldn't be farmers. You're not going to believe there's a crop next year. You're not going to believe you can do certain things. You wouldn't do what we do every day.

JESUS MAKES US DO STUFF

Other young people I spoke with said Jesus made a difference in their lives because he makes them do stuff, in particular, the "right things." One young person gave this example: "In my Latin class, I hate cheating. Everyone does it. Now people know me as this girl who won't cheat." Adolescents also said Jesus makes them do devotional times and "think about God."

JESUS TRANSFORMS

Only 2 out of the 51 young people I spoke to at various focus groups talked about Jesus making a difference in their lives by transforming them in some way. One talked about how her attitude changed when, after having a "really bad month," she discovered Jesus gave her everything she'd asked for. Another shared how seeing acts in his life that were "obviously by Jesus" changed every aspect of it.

To be sure, I was discouraged by how few teens were able to identify significant differences Jesus made in their lives. Despite being discouraged, I was not, however, surprised. Given how pervasively the teens I spoke with believed that following Jesus meant doing "churchy" things, it's no wonder Jesus doesn't appear to make much difference in their daily lives. How can he, when teens have largely confined Jesus to the walls of the church, which is not the place where they live most of their lives.

ELIMINATE THE WALLS

One key to helping teens better understand the difference Jesus makes in their daily lives is, therefore, to eliminate church walls. Blur the boundaries between church and the rest of their lives in order to help them learn to follow Jesus not just on Sundays and Wednesdays, but also throughout the rest of the week.

One powerful way to do this is to broaden their understanding of service. Most churched teens know that following Jesus means serving others. What they often fail to recognize is that the service they do outside of church is still an expression of their faith.

For example, many teens in my community are involved in Key Club at their high school. According to its website,

"Key Club is the oldest and largest service program for high school students. It is a student-led organization that teaches leadership through service to others. Members of the Kiwanis International family, Key Club members build themselves as they build their schools and communities."[5] Young people involved in Key Club serve in a multitude of service projects each year, within their schools and throughout their communities. Despite that, whenever I ask teens about the connection between their faith and their service in Key Club, I get blank stares followed by: "There's no connection between the two. I'm serving with school, not church."

Rather than accepting these comments at face value, let's push back. Challenge teens in your ministry to think through why there can't be a relationship between their faith in Jesus and the service they do with their schools. Together, examine key Scripture passages about serving others—particularly those found in the Gospels. Help young people understand that Jesus never limits serving the "least of these" to within the church's boundaries.

STOP MAKING ACCOUNTABILITY EXCLUSIVELY ABOUT SIN

Another way of blurring the boundaries between Sunday and the rest of the week is to give your youth applications that go beyond "read your Bible" or "pray more." Every time you open the Bible, wrestle with how your youth might apply that particular passage to their lives at home, work, and school. Then follow up with them the next week to see if the youth did this. Give teens a chance to reflect on how they experienced Jesus in the midst of trying to live out the passage in question.

To further formalize this, redefine accountability. In chapter 6, I shared with you how detrimental traditional accountability groups have been in my life and in the lives of other adult Christians I know. I think it's safe to say they can be even more harmful to teenagers—especially to guys.

Consider for a moment the set of questions that most accountability groups for teenage boys use:

1. How often have you looked at porn this week?
2. How often have you masturbated?
3. When did you last lust after someone?
4. Have you gone further than you should have with your girlfriend?
5. How else have you sinned this week?

How can such questions do anything other than make someone feel like a failure? How can such questions do anything other than make someone feel guilty or inadequate?

They can't.

Rather than help young people turn their eyes to Jesus, the author and perfecter of our faith, such questions turn our attention inward, toward ourselves and our sin. Rather than equip us to do God's kingdom work in community with others, such questions make us retreat into ourselves, paralyzed by guilt and shame. That is, I believe, the opposite of what we intend when we establish accountability groups in the first place.

After all, being accountable means being responsible to someone for some action. Such a definition actually implies community and dependence on one another, two things that are vitally important to the formation of a consequential faith. Knowing this, let's rethink accountability groups.

To do this, wrestle with how asking one another tough questions might challenge teens to grow as followers of Jesus. Then, together with your teens, discuss this question: "In order to help each other grow as followers of Christ, what questions might it be good for us to ask one other?"

When I did this with my student leaders, we came up with the following questions:

1. What are you doing on your own to grow closer to Jesus?
2. How have you followed Jesus outside of church this week? What was challenging about that? What was life-giving?
3. How have you applied what we talked about last week to your life this week?

Unlike your typical set of accountability questions, such questions focus not on our failures, but on Jesus. They focus on what we're doing well in our faith journeys—not on what we're doing wrong. As a result, they simultaneously encourage young people "toward love and good deeds" (Hebrews 10:24), while also challenging them to grow in their faith.

DO MORE THAN PRAY

Yet another way of encouraging youth to live out their faith in Jesus every day is to challenge them to incorporate it into their decision-making processes.

To do this, take time to study what Scripture says about plans. As a youth ministry, re-examine the commonly quoted Jeremiah 29:11, which says, " 'For I know the plans I have for you,' declares the Lord, 'plans to prosper you and not to harm you, plans to give you hope and a future.' " Help young people understand that contextually, this verse is about God's plans for the community of Israel, not individuals. Too often we forget that and instead, we make this verse about us. We chase after God's *one* plan for each of us as individuals, convinced that if we stray from that, we'll lose God's favor. Along the way, we forget how vital we are to the larger community of faith (and it to us). Far from reminding us of God's goodness and care for entire *communities* of individuals, this verse becomes a binding chain for individuals.

As you challenge teens to integrate their faith into their decision-making process, expand your study of Scripture to include more than Jeremiah 29:11. Also explore what Proverbs says about the plans of individuals. Consider, for example, the following verses:

- Our plans fail with a "lack of counsel." (Proverbs 15:22)
- If we commit our work to the Lord, "he will establish [our] plans." (Proverbs 16:3)
- Our hearts make plans, but "the Lord establishes [our] steps." (Proverbs 16:9)
- We make a lot of plans, but "the Lord's purpose prevails." (Proverbs 19:21)
- Plans are established by taking advice, so we should "gain guidance." (Proverbs 20:18)

As you explore the aforementioned passages, wrestle with what Scripture seems to suggest about the role of communities of faith in decision-making.

When you know teens are facing decisions, do more than pray. Invite teens to share about the decisions they're facing, regardless of how large or small they are. Challenge them to consider the question: *What does my faith in Jesus say about whatever it is I'm considering?*

Then experiment with communal decision-making. I was first introduced to this several years ago when a friend and mentor shared with me the process his small group used to reach decisions. Whenever someone in that group faced a major decision, they brought it before the group. The group then spent time together discussing the impending decision. Individually, they committed to praying about the decision. They then reconvened. A person only moved forward with a decision if the group discerned it was best, that it was what God was calling someone to do. Though I can't be sure of this, I suspect that had my husband and I had the courage to submit some of our past decisions to our small-group community, concerns would have been raised that would have saved us from making some costly mistakes ranging from where to purchase a home to which jobs to take.

In light of this, I can't help but wonder how such a process might also benefit teens. In addition to potentially saving teens from making costly mistakes, it would give teens the opportunity to do as Proverbs 20:18 suggests and "gain guidance" from their parents and other godly men and women, as well other teens seeking to follow Jesus. It might also give them the opportunity to encounter Christ and his wisdom in and through other people, provided those in the group are consistently turning the conversations and prayers back to Jesus. Such a process would show them in very real and tangible ways how Jesus makes a difference in their lives.

TEACH TEENS TO LISTEN

Of course, for teens to experience the difference Jesus makes in their lives through a communal discernment process, they must know how to see and hear him. Despite the fact that many youth ministries both model prayer and teach young people how to pray, the reality is that this is often hard for teens to do. As one teen I spoke with said, "It's hard to hear [Jesus] in my life and interpret what he's trying to say." If teens can't hear Jesus, then how can he possibly make a difference in their lives?

Perhaps one reason why teens find it difficult to hear Jesus is because we haven't taught them how. Instead, we've focused all our efforts on teaching them how to talk. As a result, teens know how to pray. What they don't know how to do is listen for responses to their prayers.

To remedy this, return to Scripture. Together with teens, explore the different ways Jesus and God speak throughout Scripture. Use the story of Saul's conversion in Acts 9 to wrestle with how Jesus speaks through visions. Read Psalm 46:1-3 and 10 to talk about what it means to hear God in the stillness. Then wrestle with how our constant state of busyness might prevent us from hearing Jesus. Study Elijah's encounter on Mount Horeb in 1 Kings 19:11-13 and wrestle with how God speaks through sheer silence. Introduce teens to Hannah and her longing to have a child in 1 Samuel 1:9-11. Then talk about how God speaks to us through pain. Dig deeper into Hannah's story in 1 Samuel 1:13-17 in order to further explore the role community plays in helping people hear God.

Once you've explored the different ways Jesus and God speak to people in Scripture, incorporate some of these different elements into your youth ministry. Use silence, contemplative prayer experiences, and experiential prayer stations to give teens the opportunity to practice not only talking to Jesus, but listening to him as well. Then give them the opportunity to share how they've heard God during those activities.

Ultimately, the goal in doing this is to show teens it's possible to hear God—and in particular, Jesus—in a variety of ways. In essence, it gives teens permission to experience Jesus in ways that may differ from their friends, parents, or even pastors. This, in turn, enables them to see the difference Jesus makes in multiple areas of their lives, not just in the lives they live within the walls of the church.

WRESTLE WITH IDENTITY

As I listened to young people describe the difference Jesus makes in their lives, it quickly became clear that another thing that inhibits them from understanding this is how busy and chaotic their lives are. Teens today are constantly on the move. They live in a pressure cooker that defines their worth by academic, athletic, and musical successes.

Given this, there is arguably no greater difference Jesus can make in the lives of teens than to give them a new identity, to redefine their worth. Yet, not one teen I interviewed identified this as one of the differences Jesus makes in their lives, despite the fact that pastors and youth workers think they're helping to instill this new identity in them. According to one pastor I spoke with:

> I always emphasize [to our confirmands] that their identity comes from being baptized into Christ. It's not what their friends say about them. We do a lot of emphasizing of Jesus' respect, love, and forgiveness; a lot of emphasis on Jesus. God does win that victory over death and everything that threatens us. That's integral to our understanding of [being] marked with the cross forever.

To help teens better understand their identities in Christ, explore Jesus' relationship with Peter. Talk about what an idiot Peter was—how often he spoke without thinking; how he never quite understood what was going on; how despite this, he was incredibly arrogant; and how once Jesus even called him Satan. Then talk about how in spite of all of this, Jesus gave Peter a new identity based not on what he did or didn't do, but on whose he was. Talk about how Peter then lived into this new identity, slowly becoming "the rock" Jesus said he'd be. To make this even more concrete, talk about the new names that

Jesus will one day give each of us. Since Revelation 2:17 says these names will be given to people on stones, give each of your young people a stone with a new name on it that in some way reflects who they are in Christ.

Another way to help teens understand their identities in Christ is by having them make masks. Have your group paint or decorate masks in a way that reflects who they each are. Typically, individuals will depict things that represent what they do. Once done, invite the teens to share their masks with one another. Then ask how they think Jesus would decorate their masks based on how he sees them.

After giving them time to share their thoughts, take time to explore what the Bible says about who we are because of our relationship with Jesus. In particular, study these identity statements:

- I am the salt of the earth. (Matthew 5:13)
- I am the light of the world. (Matthew 5:14)
- I am a child of God. (John 1:12)
- I am Jesus' friend. (John 15:15)
- I am chosen by Jesus to bear fruit. (John 15:5-8)
- I am a temple—a dwelling place of God. (1 Corinthians 6:17,19)
- I am a new person. My past is forgiven and everything is new. (2 Corinthians 5:17)
- I am a saint, a holy person. (Ephesians 1:1; Colossians 1:2)
- I am a citizen of heaven with all of God's family. (Ephesians 2:19)
- I am God's building project, his handiwork, created in Christ to do his work. (Ephesians 2:10)

After exploring the aforementioned identity statements, invite teens to share which of these statements they most relate to, along with which of these statements they have the hardest time believing. Then find ways to consistently remind teens of who they are in Christ.

KNOW THAT YOU ARE HIS

For years, my youth ministry has been closely involved with the refugee community. Having been forced to flee from their homelands for fear of their lives, refugees are people who've been robbed of their very basic identities. Aside from having no homes, their ethnic identities are often the very reason they've faced persecution.

Recently, a Congolese refugee told me, "Who I am is not a crime."

Despite the atrocities this woman had faced—and there were many—she understood that her identity was not the way others perceived or persecuted her ethnicity; it was, first and foremost, rooted in her relationship with Jesus. Because of her relationship with him, she knew who she was: a beloved child of God.

Ultimately, this is what I want teens to know and understand. Like the apostle John—the one whom Jesus loved—and like this Congolese woman, I want them to recognize that their identities are no longer based on what they do, but on whose they are. Truly knowing, understanding, and believing that will make an incredible difference in their lives.

I know, because it's made an incredible difference in mine.

CHAPTER NOTES

1. Kenda Creasy Dean, *Almost Christian: What the Faith of Our Teenagers Is Telling the American Church* (New York: Oxford University Press, 2010), 154.
2. Christian Smith and Patricia Snell, *Souls in Transition: The Religious and Spiritual Lives of Emerging Adults* (New York: Oxford University Press, 2009), 83, 145.
3. Ibid., 153.
4. Ibid., 154.
5. Kiwanis International, Key Club, FAQ Page, www.keyclub.org/discover/faqs.aspx.

CHAPTER 11

JESUS: OUR HOPE

Sometimes, everything seems hopeless.

Throughout the world, wars rage.

In the United States from December 2012 to June 2014, there were 15 school shootings, or approximately one every five weeks.[1] Today's teens are just as familiar with lockdown drills as they are with fire alarms.

And, at least according to some, the church is on the verge of collapse. Worship attendance in the United States is declining and most churches are shrinking, not growing.

Darkness abounds and the world seems bleak. Sometimes it feels as though Satan, not Jesus, has emerged victorious.

THE HOPE FOUND IN SCRIPTURE

Despite this, today's teens appear hopeful. A whopping 89 percent of the adolescents I surveyed agreed with the statement, "My faith in Jesus gives me hope."

Certainly, that's encouraging. Yet, as with other trends we've explored in this book, further digging suggests this may not actually be the good news it first appears to be. That such a large percentage of young people agree their faith in Jesus gives them hope means that many do so even though they don't believe Jesus is God. In fact, of those who say Jesus gives them hope, less than half (45 percent) also affirm Jesus is God.

Such a view of hope runs contrary to what Scripture describes:

- Hope comes from Christ. (1 Corinthians 15:19)
- Hope is the result of suffering and perseverance. (Romans 5:3-5)
- Hope is connected to faith and love. (1 Corinthians 13:13)
- Hope is living. (1 Peter 1:3)

Such a hope is lasting and enduring, capable of carrying us through troubled times.

In contrast, a hope found in a Jesus who isn't God won't last. Eventually, it will collapse; and when it does, the faith of teens will be its casualty. To help you see what I mean, let's return to some of the archetypes of Jesus found in chapter 1. What does hope in each of these archetypes look like? When and how does it break down?

HOPE IN SUPERHERO JESUS

Hope in Superhero Jesus is powerful because superheroes are inherently powerful. Through Superhero Jesus we have hope that ultimately, good will triumph over bad. We believe that in a time of crisis, Superhero Jesus will show up and conquer our enemies. What we're less sure of is if Superhero Jesus will stay after the crisis is over. We question whether or not he'll remain present with us in our everyday, ordinary lives, where most of life is lived. Our hope in Superhero Jesus wanes whenever we confront small problems, the kind we convince ourselves superheroes don't have time for.

HOPE IN MR. ROGERS JESUS

Mr. Rogers Jesus gives us hope for a better world. In him, we have hope that one person *can* make a difference in the life of another through simple acts of kindness. The problem is, such hope is only temporary. Mr. Rogers Jesus is simply too nice to confront the real injustices in our world. As Rick Lawrence says in *Jesus-Centered Youth Ministry*: "Mr. Rogers is a pleasant enough guy, but you wouldn't follow him into a dark alley full of street thugs waiting to beat you up."[2] So it is with Mr. Rogers Jesus. He makes a good neighbor but not a good leader. We have no hope or expectation he'll ever put an end to world hunger, genocides, or other grave injustices.

HOPE IN GODLIKE JESUS

Similar to our hope in Superhero Jesus, our hope in Godlike Jesus is rooted in his power. In Godlike Jesus, we have hope that all will one day be made right. Godlike Jesus is, after all, a higher power capable of performing miracles. The problem is, since Godlike Jesus isn't necessarily God, we fear his power may be limited. There may be some things that are simply more powerful than he is, and as a result, as much as he may want to, he cannot fix everything. We're disappointed when Godlike Jesus acts in a way that runs contrary to our expectations of him. What's more, since Godlike Jesus is otherworldly, we have no hope of ever relating to or understanding him.

HOPE IN SPIRITUAL GURU JESUS

Our hope in Spiritual Guru Jesus is on par with the hope we might have in a pastor or therapist. We hope such people will provide us with greater understanding about ourselves and the world around us so we, in turn, can change. We know, however, that any change we experience comes from within. Spiritual Guru Jesus may have a special relationship with God, but since he's not God himself, ultimately, he cannot change anything.

HOPE IN JOE JESUS

Joe Jesus gives us relational hope. In Joe Jesus we have a very real, relatable friend who we hope will weather the storms of life with us. Like Spiritual Guru Jesus, Joe Jesus gives us new insights into our problems. And while these insights may be helpful, in reality, we know he's just like us. Therefore, Joe

Jesus can't fix anything we can't remedy ourselves.

HOPE IN KING JESUS

In King Jesus, we have hope that systemic injustices will one day be fixed. Yet, we also know King Jesus reigns through power. Unfortunately, the world around us has taught us that power sometimes corrupts. So we fear that King Jesus might someday become Dictator Jesus, concerned not with the welfare of his people, but with his own interests. As a result, uncertain as to whether or not Jesus is actually God, we lack hope that King Jesus' power will be tempered with compassion and ultimately used for good.

HOPE IN ORTHODOX JESUS

In contrast, our hope in Orthodox Jesus—the one who is also God—is complete. In him, power meets compassion; distance meets the incarnation. Through him, we have hope that ultimately good will triumph over bad. Through the cross we know death has been defeated, and through his resurrection we believe that even now he is redeeming the world and making all things right. He alone has the power and authority to end the injustices that surround us, yet he's called and equipped us to be part of his mission. We have, therefore, hope for a better world.

Although he is powerful, in Jesus we also have the hope of a relationship. Through the incarnation, we're able to relate to Jesus, and he to us. Because of this relationship, we trust that what matters to us, matters to him; that what matters to him, also shapes us. Beyond that, we have the promise of Jesus' presence. We trust he'll stay long after a crisis abates and that we'll powerfully encounter him not just in the extraordinary moments of our lives, but also in the ordinary ones.

JESUS IS MY HOPE

Even though we know this, my experience in my own youth

ministry, as well as in my congregational visits for this research, suggests that while it's easy to talk about how Jesus is our hope from a hypothetical, abstract standpoint, it's much harder to do so in concrete, personal ways. Yet, the reality is it's much easier for young people to believe Jesus is their hope when they see and hear how he's given others hope in their lives.

About a year ago, I profoundly experienced the hope of Jesus in my own life when I suffered a miscarriage. That experience ushered me into the darkest period of my life and into a pain I've never known before. It happened during Holy Week, and as a result, I found myself pondering Jesus and the cross in new ways.

Prior to that experience, I knew and wholeheartedly believed Jesus died for our sins. Since then, however, I've become increasingly convinced that's not all Jesus did on the cross. When we reduce the cross to a mere transaction—his death for our sins—I now believe we miss the greater story.

Christians speak often of the incarnation and of how, through Jesus' birth, God became like us, coming to dwell among us. Certainly, that's true. But for me, in the year since my miscarriage, the place where I've come to most see Jesus' humanity and divinity is not in his birth, but rather in his death. It's in the moment when he cried out in anguish from the cross, "My God, my God, why have you forsaken me?" (Matthew 27:46; Mark 15:34).

As we discussed in chapter 4, Jesus' crucifixion was necessary to save us from our sins and to conquer death. But what I now understand is that it was also necessary for God to know the pain that's inherently a part of the human experience. In the midst of my darkest hours when God felt unapproachable, Jesus didn't.

While it's true Jesus represents us to God, in the midst of my miscarriage, I realized that on the cross, Jesus also represents God to us. In essence, the cross pleads God's case to us every time we question: *Why does he allow bad things to happen to good people?*

Today, the cross is important to me because it's the crux of my faith. Beyond that, however, it gives me permission to mourn—to cry, scream, and wail against God and the injustices of this world. It allows me to not only mourn Jesus' death, but to name my own grief as well as the grief my youth carry.

What last year taught me is that as much as the cross is about death, it's also about life; as much as it's about paying a penalty, it's also about redemption. Through Jesus' death and resurrection, I know beyond a shadow of a doubt that Jesus *is* God. I also know he's not a distant God. Instead, he's a God who's with us in the thick of things. He dwells with us in the darkness and, eventually, carries us to the light.

As a result of my experience with miscarriage, I can now say with certainty that my faith in Jesus gives me hope. In fact, Jesus *is* my hope.

JESUS IS *OUR* HOPE

Having experienced the power of hope in Jesus in my own life, I want desperately for my youth to be able to confidently say their faith in Jesus also gives them hope, regardless of what valleys they find themselves in either presently or in the future.

I'm sure you want that too.
But the truth is, even though most young people say their faith in Jesus gives them hope, chances are good that because their Christologies are so weak, when darkness confronts them, this hope—and their faith in Jesus—will crumble rather than carry them. To prevent this from happening, their faith must

be rooted in the real, Orthodox Jesus, not in a one-dimensional caricature of him. As youth workers, that means nothing we do in ministry matters more than instilling a strong Christology in our teens, the kind we've talked about throughout this book.

Without Jesus, there is no hope. The church is dead and Satan has won. In contrast, with Jesus, no matter how much evidence exists to the contrary, the church—his body—will prevail. With Jesus, there is always hope—in the face of miscarriage, war, school shootings, and in whatever other situations we, and our young people, find ourselves.

In all of them, Jesus *is* hope.

CHAPTER NOTES

1. Ashley Fantz, Lindsey Knight, and Kevin Wang, "A Closer Look: How Many Newtown-Like School Shootings Since Sandy Hook?" *CNN.com*, CNN U.S., updated June 19, 2014, www.cnn.com/2014/06/11/us/school-shootings-cnn-number/.
2. Rick Lawrence, *Jesus-Centered Youth Ministry* (Loveland, CO: Group Publishing, 2007), 32.

CHAPTER 12

JESUS: THE FOUNDATION OF OUR FAITH

Four months after I began serving a new church as its youth worker, I was engulfed in a bitter conflict.

The teens in my youth ministry—in particular, the seniors—hated me.

Why?

Because I had the audacity to make them open the Bible and talk about Jesus.

I shouldn't have been surprised. After all, from the start this senior class told me, "We use the Bibles as doorstops in the youth room."

I thought they were joking.

It turns out they were serious.

Our conflict eventually led to several meetings. As this group described their vision for our youth ministry, it became clear to me that what they wanted was not a youth ministry, but a community center: a place to go in their free time, hang out, talk about anything they wanted to (as long as it wasn't Jesus), and play games.

After hearing their vision, I was asked, "Could you live with that? What's so wrong with having a place teens want to come to?"

To which I responded, "Nothing, if you're a YMCA or a park district."

I went on to explain how I thought there was something very wrong with a church that was satisfied with merely being a place teens wanted to go.

After all, Jesus is what makes us unique from every other place there is. How could any church ministry not be centered around him?

CHURCHES WITHOUT JESUS

I wish I could say I'm the only youth worker who's ever had a conversation like that one. Unfortunately, I know I'm not. Other studies suggest a great number of youth ministries look far more like non-faith-based organizations than they do the traditional church.

For example, in 1972, Dean Kelly found that "youth of liberal/mainline denominations were barely able to identify themselves as 'Christian' let alone articulate it or see faith as having any relevance to their lives."[1] Since then, other research has drawn similar conclusions. In *Youth Ministry in a Multifaith Society*, Len Kageler says a study based in Melbourne, Australia, found "Protestant youth workers seemed less concerned about theological foundations and more concerned about 'doing something.' "[2]

Kageler—a youth ministry researcher, practitioner, and professor—writes: "Many churches and their Christian youth ministries happily affirm their Christian faith but also affirm there are other equally valid ways to know God."[3]

In light of these findings, perhaps it shouldn't surprise us that the massive exodus of people from the church is a frequent topic of conversation in the Christian world. The day before

I wrote this chapter, a *Christianity Today* article entitled "Dropouts and Disciples: How Many Students Are Really Leaving the Church?" caught my attention. According to LifeWay Research and article author Ed Stetzer:

> Eighty percent of young people who dropped out of church said they did not plan to do so during high school. It's not that most rejected the church. Our teenagers aren't primarily leaving because they have significant disagreements with their theological upbringings or out of some sense of rebellion. For the most part, they simply lose track of the church and stop seeing it as important to their [lives].[4]

As a practicing youth worker, I find such research interesting and to some degree, helpful. How can we get people to stay in the church if we don't know why they're leaving?

As a researcher and a Christian, though, I can't help but wonder if we're asking the wrong question. Why is it that we're more concerned with people leaving the church than we are with the church leaving Jesus?

WOULD JESUS ATTEND YOUR CHURCH?

In case you're not convinced the church is leaving Jesus, consider this: Teens who are active in their churches today are unsure about not only who Jesus is, but also his relationship with the church. When asked if Jesus would attend their churches if he were on earth today, most teens I spoke with said no. When I asked teens why they thought this, here's what I heard:

> "[Jesus is] keeping his distance [from the church] because he's frustrated—church attendance is down across the world."
> "Every single church is wrong in some aspect. No

church has got down the exact details of everything correctly. Jesus wouldn't go into that church and be a member of that church."

"[Jesus] wouldn't be a member of any one denomination. That would be inconsistent with his nature. He'd be welcoming of anyone willing to welcome the idea of God."

"I don't think church is what Jesus wanted it to be."

"[Jesus'] relationship with the church is bad. He doesn't go there."

"[Jesus] never got along with the church."

"You can't say Jesus is here and not in a crack house. He's not only in churches."

The massive popularity of Jefferson Bethke's 2012 spoken word video, "Why I Hate Religion, but Love Jesus," suggests the teens I spoke to are not the only ones who think Jesus wouldn't attend their churches.[5] The prevailing mindset in today's teens seems to be that Jesus would rather be anywhere but the church. To them, this isn't because Jesus abandoned the church; it's because the church has abandoned Jesus.

IMAGINE A CHURCH WITHOUT ...

Imagine, for a moment, what the ramifications are of a faith—and church—without Jesus.

Since Christ Jesus himself is "the cornerstone," a church without Jesus is, quite simply, no longer a church (Ephesians 2:20). It's like a country club without a golf course. It's nothing more than a community center that's a wonderful place for good people to meet.

208

Since "the wages of sin is death" without Jesus, there would be no salvation, no hope of eternal life; there would only be our impending death (Romans 6:23). Beyond that, without Jesus, there would be no "abundant" life in the here and now; there would only be the indulgent life (John 10:10 NKJV). Without Jesus, as individuals and communities, we'd lack identity. Rather than define ourselves according to whose we are, we'd only be able to define ourselves according to what we do.

Such a picture of life, faith, and church is, at least to me, dismal. Yet, I fear that based on my research, this is precisely where the church is headed.

Unless, of course, we do something to stop it; unless we recommit ourselves—and our ministries—to Jesus, who offers us a countercultural way of life that allows us to intimately know God the Father (John 14:7); an example of servanthood that is, in fact, a radical expression of power; and the greatest expression of love the world has ever known (John 15:12-14).

So, my friends, go forth.

In all you do, remember that Jesus is the one on whom "Christianity stands or falls."[6] So in all you do, make him— not games, relationships, camps, or even mission trips—the focal point of your ministry. Boldly proclaim the truth that Jesus is both fully God and fully human. Affirm his perfection. Courageously proclaim that he alone is the way to both eternal life later and abundant life now.

Model what it means to prioritize not just church but Jesus, in every aspect of your life. Invest in the christological formation of parents, even when it's hard. Challenge teens (and their families) to be countercultural enough to boldly share their faith in Christ. Equip them to be part of God's kingdom work both within your congregation and your community. Then commission and release them to be agents of change knowing that this Jesus thing matters—not just to you, but to them and to the world around us.

After all, it's Jesus that makes a difference in our lives. It's Jesus that gives us hope.

CHAPTER NOTES

1. Len Kageler, *Youth Ministry in a Multifaith Society: Forming Christian Identity Among Skeptics, Syncretists and Sincere Believers of Other Faiths* (Downers Grove, IL: InterVarsity Press, 2014), 86.

2. Ibid., 89.

3. Ibid., 94.

4. Ed Stetzer, "Dropouts and Disciples: How Many Students Are Really Leaving the Church?" *The Exchange* (blog), *Christianity Today*, posted May 14, 2014, www.christianitytoday.com/edstetzer/2014/may/dropouts-and-disciples-how-many-students-are-really-leaving.html.

5. Jefferson Bethke, "Why I Hate Religion, But Love Jesus," Spoken Word Video, www.youtube.com/watch?v=1IAhDGYlpqY.

6. Carl E. Braaten, *Who Is Jesus? Disputed Questions and Answers* (Grand Rapids, MI: William B. Eerdmans Publishing Co, 2011), 5.

APPENDIX A

THE JESUS GAP RESEARCH OVERVIEW

The Jesus Gap is based on a qualitative, grounded theory study I conducted from July 2012 through March 2013 as my master's thesis at Huntington University under the guidance of Dr. Dave Rahn.

My research was driven by the primary question: "What is the nature of the christological understanding of high school students in the Evangelical Lutheran Church of America (ELCA)?" Additional questions that drove this study included:

- What factors (both people and practices) contribute to high school students' understanding of Christ?
- How do high school students' Christologies affect how they live out their faith in the world around them?
- What practices would contribute to a better understanding of who Christ is among high school students in the ELCA?

High school students in the ELCA served as the primary unit of analysis for this study because it's the context in which I currently serve as a youth worker.

The study included two major parts: a large survey and site visits at four representative congregations within the ELCA. Due to the study's scope, the survey was limited to questions directly related to Jesus. Questions were divided into four parts. The first part of the survey solicited basic demographic information from each respondent, using language commonly employed by the ELCA. The second part of the survey asked young people to choose one word each from a series of

10-word pairs that described Jesus. The third part of the survey asked young people multiple-choice questions about Jesus, as well as questions about how frequently they talked about him and who influenced their perceptions of him. The fourth part of the survey asked youth to respond to three short-answer questions about Jesus.

At each site visit, I observed a program, conducted separate focus groups for youth and their parents, and interviewed youth workers and pastors. To increase the study's validity, I analyzed each part independently of one another.

PARTICIPANTS

Surveys were completed by 369 high school students in the ELCA. Of those young people, 300 were surveyed at the ELCA's 2012 National Youth Gathering, a number that represented just over 1 percent of the total 25,000 high school students who attended the event. Sixty-nine additional youth were surveyed from four different participating research congregations. All total, surveyed youth came from 16 different states including Colorado, Iowa, Illinois, Indiana, Maryland, Michigan, Minnesota, Nebraska, New Jersey, New Mexico, North Carolina, Ohio, Pennsylvania, Texas, Washington, and Wisconsin. (See Figure 13.)

Female adolescents totaled 58 percent , and 41 percent were male. Of all those surveyed, 1 percent were 13 years old; 43 percent were 14 to 15 years old; 43 percent were 16 to 17 years old; and 12 percent were 18 to 20 years old. As far as race, 95 percent of the youth surveyed were white. Though such a statistic is somewhat disappointing, it is not surprising. Instead, it reflects the demographics of the ELCA, which according to the churchwide office is 94.66 percent white.

The vast majority of young people surveyed had grown up in their congregations: 42 percent had attended for 15 to 19 years; 28 percent had attended for 10 to 14 years; 15 percent had attended for 6 to 9 years; 10 percent had attended for 2 to 5 years; and 4 percent had attended for 1 year. (See Figure 14.)

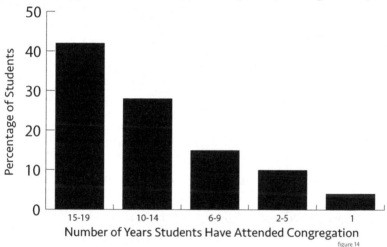

figure 14

Four ELCA congregations also participated in this research project. To choose them, I asked rostered ELCA church workers to recommended congregations from across the country with active youth ministries. This generated a list of 33 potential research congregations. I then chose four that allowed for a diverse sample in terms of size, synodical affiliation, and geographic (suburban versus rural) demographics.

PROCEDURE

In order to gain access to a large population of high school students in the ELCA from various parts of the country all at once, I surveyed an initial wave of 300 high school students from around the country at the ELCA's triennial Youth Gathering. The Youth Gathering limited the survey sample to high school students in the ELCA. Consequently, convenience sampling was used to obtain 300 anonymous responses to christological surveys from people of various genders and ethnicities, as well as from different locations within the United States. High school students from my youth ministry assisted in collecting surveys from teens at the Youth Gathering.

Since this study's theoretical framework was grounded theory, I analyzed data throughout it. This allowed each phase of the study to build upon previously collected data. As I analyzed results from the Youth Gathering surveys, I simultaneously conducted site visits at the four research congregations. Each congregation involved in this part of the study:

- Distributed and collected consent forms prior to my site visit
- Distributed and collected completed christological surveys
- Arranged a schedule for me that included
  - A 30-minute one-on-one interview with the senior pastor
  - A separate, 60-minute one-on-one interview with the lead youth worker
  - A 60-minute focus group with parents of high school students
  - A separate, 60-minute focus group with high school students
  - The opportunity to observe worship or a youth ministry program (Note: To allow focus group

participants to be as honest as possible, neither the pastor nor the youth worker were allowed to attend them.)

Using all previous waves of data, I then formulated a standardized open-ended interview. This allowed responses from each congregation to easily be compared with one another. A different, albeit similar, open-ended interview was used for each distinct sample population (pastors, youth workers, parents, and young people). Each interview contained some questions used at every site, as well as others prompted by additional waves of data. The goal of these questions was to gain a better understanding of adolescents' responses to the survey questions, clarify their Christologies, and understand what factors contributed to the development of those Christologies.

Once all data was entered, coded, and analyzed, it was interpreted in several ways. Results from each congregation were interpreted independently of one another in order to sketch the Christology of teens in a given congregation. Data from each congregation was also compared with one another and with that from the denomination (Youth Gathering data plus data from all research congregations) as a whole. Finally, data from the denomination as a whole was compared to both evangelical and Lutheran Christologies.

APPENDIX B
SURVEYS AND QUESTIONS

CHRISTOLOGY SURVEY

First, we'd like to get some information about you. Circle all that apply.

Male
Female
Transgendered

13 years old
14-15 years old
16-17 years old
18-20 years old

African American/Black
American Indian/Native Alaskan
Latino/Spanish
Asian/Pacific Islander
Arabic/Middle Eastern
Multi-ethnic
White
Other

Where is your church? (*Town, State ZIP*)

How many years have you been attending your church?
Less than 1
2-5
6-9
10-14
15-19
Prior to attending your church, did you attend another?

Yes
No

If yes, which denomination was your former church a part of?

Methodist
Presbyterian
Catholic
Baptist
Bible Church
UCC
Nondenominational
ELCA
Evangelical Free
I don't know.

Other:

Next, we'd like to find out what you believe about Jesus. No one will judge your responses. We just want to know what you honestly believe.

Check which word from each pair best describes Jesus.

Pair 1: Nice   Rowdy
Pair 2: Wise   Foolish
Pair 3: Obedient   Rebellious
Pair 4: Strong   Weak
Pair 5: Fun   Boring
Pair 6: Emotional   Unfeeling
Pair 7: Talkative   Quiet
Pair 8: Calm   Angry
Pair 9: Devoted   Uncommitted
Pair 10: Conventional   Revolutionary

For each question below, circle the answer that best describes your current understanding of Jesus.

Was Jesus fully human?
Yes   No   I don't know.

Is Jesus God?
Yes   No   I don't know.

Was Jesus perfect?
Yes   No   I don't know.

Did Jesus sin?
Yes   No   I don't know.

Did Jesus perform miracles?

Yes   No   I don't know.

Did Jesus rise from the dead?
Yes   No   I don't know.

Is it possible to be a Christian and not believe in Jesus?
Yes   No   I don't know.

How frequently do you talk about **Jesus** (not just God)...

... In your youth ministry?
Every time we meet   Weekly   Monthly   Yearly   Never

... With your friends?
Every time we meet   Weekly   Monthly   Yearly   Never

... With your family?
Every time we meet   Weekly   Monthly   Yearly   Never

How important is your faith to you?
Very   Somewhat   Not very   Irrelevant

How important is Jesus to your faith?

Very   Somewhat   Not very   Irrelevant

My faith in Jesus helps me find meaning and purpose in life.

Agree   Disagree

My faith in Jesus gives me hope.

Agree   Disagree

Rank the following from 1 to 6 according to who or what
has most influenced your understanding of Jesus. (1 = Most
influential; 6 = Least influential)

Parent(s):   Youth Pastor/Director:

Pastor(s):   Friend(s):

Media: Scripture:

**Now that you've been thinking about Jesus, here's a chance
to answer a few questions in your own words. Answer each
question below with 1 to 2 sentences. There is no right or
wrong answer to these questions; we simply want to know
what you believe.**

Who is Jesus?

What did Jesus teach?

Why did Jesus die?

INITIAL INTERVIEW QUESTIONS FOR PASTORS

What are your most foundational beliefs about Jesus?

How important is Jesus to your faith? Why?

Who or what has influenced your beliefs about Jesus?

How do your own beliefs about Jesus impact your ministry?

How frequently do you talk about Jesus (not just God) in worship?

How frequently do you talk about Jesus (not just God) in Bible studies or conversations with parishioners?

When you talk about Jesus, what do you typically say about him?

Which, if any, do you emphasize more: Jesus' humanity or his divinity? Why?

How might your emphasis of Jesus' humanity or divinity impact the development of your parishioners' Christologies?

Aside from what you say about Jesus, how else do you go about developing the Christologies of your parishioners?

A survey of 300 students at the Youth Gathering revealed that 45 percent of students surveyed believe Jesus is God and 44 percent believe he isn't. Does this surprise you? Why or why not?

How indicative do you think this statistic would be of adults in the ELCA? Why?

When asked if it's possible to be a Christian and not believe in Jesus, of 300 young people surveyed at the Youth Gathering, 117 said no; 93 said yes; and 88 said, "I don't know." In other words, nearly two-thirds of the young people surveyed either don't know or believe you can be a Christian without believing in Jesus. Describe your reaction to this.

How indicative do you think this statistic would be of adults in the ELCA? Why?

How important do you think it is for people to understand the centrality of Jesus to the Christian faith?

Aside from the church, who or what do you think influences your parishioners' beliefs about Jesus?

What do you hope those in your congregation know/believe about Jesus? Why?

INITIAL INTERVIEW QUESTIONS FOR YOUTH WORKERS

What are your most foundational beliefs about Jesus?

How important is Jesus to your faith? Why?

Who or what has influenced your beliefs about Jesus?

How do your own beliefs about Jesus impact your ministry to young people?

How frequently do you talk about Jesus (not just God) in your youth ministry?

What do you typically say about Jesus in your youth ministry?

Which, if any, do you emphasize more: Jesus' humanity or his divinity? Why?

How might your emphasis of Jesus' humanity or divinity impact the development of teens' Christologies?

Aside from what you say about Jesus, how else do you go about developing the Christologies of your youth?

A survey of 300 young people at the Youth Gathering revealed that 45 percent of those surveyed believe Jesus is God and 44 percent believe he isn't. Does this surprise you? Why or why not?

How important is it for adolescents to know and believe Jesus is God? Why?

Consider your youth ministry. What, if any, steps do you take to help young people believe Jesus is God?

A survey of 300 young people at the Youth Gathering revealed that 51 percent of those surveyed believe Jesus sinned. Only 32 percent of those surveyed believe Jesus did not sin. Does this surprise you? Why or why not?

Why do you think so many young people believe Jesus sinned?

How might young people's beliefs as to whether or not Jesus sinned impact their faith?

When asked if it's possible to be a Christian and not believe in Jesus, of 300 young people surveyed at the Youth Gathering, 117 said no; 93 said yes; and 88 said I don't know. In other words, nearly two-thirds of students surveyed either don't know or believe you can be a Christian without believing in Jesus. Describe your reaction to this.

In a world that's becoming increasingly multicultural and pluralistic, how important do you think it is for adolescents to understand the centrality of Jesus to the Christian faith?

As a youth worker, how (if at all) do you emphasize the centrality of Jesus to the Christian faith?

Aside from you and your ministry, who or what do you think influences your young people's beliefs about Jesus?

By the time a student graduates from high school, what do you hope they will know/believe about Jesus? Why?

INITIAL FOCUS GROUP QUESTIONS FOR PARENTS

What words would you use to describe Jesus? Why?

Who is Jesus?

What characteristics of Jesus do you most admire? Why?

Is Jesus God? Why or why not?

What did Jesus teach?

Did Jesus practice what he preached? Why or why not?

Did Jesus sin? Why or why not?

If so, what are some examples of Jesus' sins?

Why did Jesus die?

What does it mean to follow Jesus?

What, if any, difference does Jesus make in your everyday life?

Why should someone believe in Jesus?

To you, what does it mean to be a Christian? Why?

What, if anything, must someone believe about Jesus to be a Christian?

Who or what has influenced your understanding of Jesus?

Specifically, what did you learn from your parents about Jesus?

What have you learned from your church about Jesus?

What have you taught your teens about Jesus? Why?

What do you hope your teen will learn from the church about Jesus? Why?

What impact do you hope Jesus will have in the life of your teen? Why?

INITIAL FOCUS GROUP QUESTIONS FOR HIGH SCHOOL STUDENTS

If Jesus were alive today, who do you think he would hang out with? Why?

What characteristics of Jesus do you most admire? Why?

Who or what has informed your perception of Jesus?

Specifically, what have you learned from your parents about Jesus?

What have you learned from your youth ministry about Jesus?

What have you learned from church (and in particular, Sunday morning worship) about Jesus?

What have you learned from Scripture about Jesus?

Do you think Jesus practiced what he preached? Why or why not?

Do you think Jesus sinned? Why or why not?

If so, what are some examples of Jesus' sins?

If Jesus sinned, can he still be God? Why or why not?

What does it mean to follow Jesus?

Do you think it's possible to recognize a follower of Jesus? Why or why not?

If so, how can you recognize a follower of Jesus?

What, if any, difference does Jesus make in your everyday life?

Why should someone believe in Jesus?

How can we show Jesus to others?

In John 14:6, Jesus says, "I am the way and the truth and the life. No one comes to the Father except through me." What does this mean to you?

To you, what does it mean to be a Christian? Why?

What, if anything, must someone believe about Jesus to be a Christian?

ACKNOWLEDGMENTS

Contrary to popular belief, writing doesn't happen in a vacuum. I have, without a doubt, learned that this year. Thanks to all those who have, in some way, made this book possible:

The Youth Cartel, for daring to take a chance on a new voice.

Dr. Dave Rahn and Dr. Terry Linhart, for teaching me to love research and for their guidance throughout this project.

My mentors—Kitty, Tony, Ginny, and Bob—you're why I'm still in ministry today.

The pastors at Faith—Jim and Heidi—for daily supporting not only my ministry there, but also my calling to serve the wider church.

Heidi Hagstrom and the ELCA's Youth Gathering staff, for graciously allowing me to survey young people at the 2012 Youth Gathering.

The FLY students who attended the Youth Gathering, for boldly surveying their peers.

The churches and young people who courageously allowed me to observe, survey, and interview them about their beliefs in Jesus.

My students—past, present, and future—for daily inspiring, challenging, and teaching me what it means to follow Jesus.

Rebecca, for reading every word of this book and showing me how to make it better.

Doug, for embodying Jesus to me, and—more practically—for writing the software used to analyze my research, reading early drafts, and loving me always.

Made in the
USA
Middletown, DE

76808868R00136